My brothers were ready. They held each other's hands tightly. Mother had secured my baby sister between her arms. My father strained to see the road from behind the mound of clothes and blankets he carried. But in spite of my desperate attempts to obey my parents' commands, my three-and-a-half-year-old hands were unable to lace up the one shoe I had put on. My right foot was still shoeless.

"Yamma, Yaba! Help me!" I cried in a hushed voice, lest I attract attention and we all die. But no one answered.

At that moment, a new wave of fleeing villagers rushed by. As they disappeared, everything faded into stillness. And my family was gone.

The family in *Tasting the Sky*: Mirriam and Suleiman Barakat, with their children Ibtisam, Muhammad, and Basel

TASTING THE SKY

IBTISAM BARAKAT

SQUARE
FISH

FARRAR STRAUS GIROUX
NEW YORK

SQUARE
FISH

An imprint of Macmillan Publishing Group, LLC
175 Fifth Avenue
New York, NY 10010
mackids.com

Our books may be purchased in bulk for promotional, educational, or business use.
Please contact your local bookseller or the Macmillan Corporate and Premium
Sales Department at (800) 221-7945 ext. 5442 or by e-mail at
MacmillanSpecialMarkets@macmillan.com.

Library of Congress Cataloging-in-Publication Data

Barakat, Ibtisam.
    Tasting the sky a Palestinian childhood / Ibtisam Barakat.
        p.   cm.
    ISBN 978-1-250-09718-7 (paperback)   ISBN 978-1-42999-847-5 (ebook)
    1. Arab-Israeli Conflict—Juvenile literature.   [1. Barakat, Ibtisam.   2. Children, Palestinian
Arab—Biography.]   I. Title.

DS119.7.B2845 2007
956.95.2044092—dc22
[B]

2006041265

Originally published in the United States by Farrar Straus Giroux
First Square Fish Edition: 2016
Book designed by Barbara Grzeslo
Square Fish logo designed by Filomena Tuosto

9   10

AR: 5.8 / LEXILE: 870L

Permission to include the lyrics of "Ya Dara Douri Fina" and "Salami Lakom," by the Rahbani
Brothers from the album "Jesr El Awda," has been granted by Mansour Rahbani.

An earlier version of the chapter "Shoelaces" was published by Pocket Books in 1998 under the
title "Marked for Destruction" in *Children of Israel, Children of Palestine*, edited by Laurel Holliday.
An earlier version of the chapter "Shelter" was first published by Alfred A. Knopf in 2002 under the
title "The Second Day" in the book *Shattered: Stories of Children and War*, edited by Jennifer
Armstrong.

The Sinai Peninsula, indicated as an occupied territory on the 1967 map, page viii, was
returned to Egypt in 1979.

The origin of baklava, disputed on page 9, is widely believed among food historians to be
neither Arabic nor Greek but Assyrian, dating to the eighth century. Various nations in the Middle
East claim this pastry as their own and have contributed to perfecting it.

The quotation on page 172 is primarily attributed to Philo of Alexandria (C. 20 B.C.E.–C. 50 C.E.).
However, Philo scholars continue to debate its location in his writings. Plato occasionally is credited
with having said it.

To Alef, the letter
that begins the alphabets
of both Arabic and Hebrew—
two Semitic languages,
sisters for centuries.

May we find the language
that takes us
to the only home there is—
one another's hearts.

To my parents,
Suleiman and Mirriam,
who did their best,
and to my brothers,
Basel and Muhammad,
the two heroes of my childhood.

And to children everywhere.

CONTENTS

Places key to events in *Tasting the Sky*
June 1967, after the Six-Day War

Palestinian areas under Israeli occupation

Other occupied areas

○ Depopulated village

HISTORICAL NOTE

The Middle East is a region of the world that many consider to be the cradle of civilization. Today this ancient land is struggling under the heavy weight of its history, crying out for understanding. The fight over the Holy Land, or the areas various people call Israel and Palestine, is at the heart of the current Middle East conflict.

Many wars and world events have impacted the Holy Land during the past century and have led to the current situation. These include World War I and the European colonization of the Middle East that followed; World War II, the Holocaust, and the urgent need for Jews to find a home; the subsequent creation of the State of Israel on land that was for the most part populated by Palestinian Arabs; and the wars of both 1948 and 1967, which took place between Arab countries and Israel.

The war of 1948 resulted in the establishment of the State of Israel on what used to be Palestine, leaving the West Bank, the Gaza Strip, and East Jerusalem under Arab administration. In June 1967, when the Six-Day War ended, Israel occupied the West Bank and the Gaza Strip and had taken over East Jerusalem.

The year 2007 marks the fortieth anniversary of the Six-Day War. *Tasting the Sky* is set within the framework of that war and the Israeli occupation that followed. Part I, "A Letter to No One," takes place in 1981 and leads to remembering the Six-Day War. Part II, "The Postal Box of Memory," begins on the first day of the Six-Day War and spans four years, ending in 1971. Part III, "A Letter to Everyone," takes the reader back to 1981.

The conflict between Israelis and Palestinians is one of the most difficult of modern times because both peoples, from inside their respective contexts, have justifiably strong attachments to the Holy Land. Reduced to its core, this conflict is about two peoples, both of whom have suffered difficult histories. A major obstacle to resolving this conflict seems to be the inability to find a common ground that would allow both sides to understand and accept each other's history and to become partners in achieving their similar goals of living in freedom and peace.

However, this is not only a struggle between two peoples. It is also an international conflict, fueled by religious and ethnic rivalries as well as a variety of economic and military interests. Many countries have an intense involvement with the Israelis and Palestinians. But the approach of siding with one group or the other, caring about only one rather than both, seems to add to the strife. Resolving this conflict is likely to require the constructive participation of many people in the world. A genuine solution must allow not only freedom and security for both Israelis and Palestinians but also room for both peoples to heal from having been victimized as well as heal from having victimized others. When achieved, this solution is sure to offer tremendous hope for all of humanity, since this conflict has become one of the great obstacles to world peace today.

To learn more about the Middle East, and to deepen our understanding of both Palestinians and Israelis, it helps to share stories. Mine is one of many. Together, these stories can show us how all people are interdependent and have the same basic needs. Together, these stories may inspire us to join hearts and minds so that, with our collective wisdom, a solution for this conflict—and any other—is possible.

Where have you been?
Why have you not grown?
If asked,
We'll say we'd forgotten.

The one who called children
To grow
Had come and gone.
To us said nothing.

—Translation from the Arabic song
"Ya Dara Douri Fina" by Fairuz,
lyrics by Rahbani Brothers

PART I

A Letter to
No One

Like a bird clawing
The bars of a cage
And wishing them branches,
My fingers grasp
The bus rails before me.

But I wish for nothing.

I'm midway from Birzeit to Ramallah, at the Israeli army checkpoint at Surda. No one knows how long our bus will stay here. An army jeep is parked sideways to block the road. Soldiers in another jeep look on with their guns. They are ready to shoot. A barrier that punctures tires stands near the stop sign. I regret that I chose to sit up front.

The window of the bus frames the roadblock like a postcard that I wish I could send to all my faraway pen pals. They ask me to describe a day in my life. But I do not dare. If I told them of the fear that hides under my feet like a land mine, would they write back?

A soldier leaps into the bus. He stands on the top step. His eyes are hidden behind sunglasses, dark like midnight. "To where?" He throws the question like a rock. I pull my head toward my body like a tortoise. If I don't see him, perhaps he won't see me.

He asks again. I stay silent. I don't think a high school girl like me is visible enough, exists enough for a soldier with a rifle, a pistol, a club, a helmet, and high boots to notice. He must be talking to the man sitting behind me.

But he leans closer. His khaki uniform and the back of his rifle touch my knee. My flesh freezes.

"To where?" He bends close to my face. I feel everyone on the bus nudging me with their anxious silence.

"Ramallah," I stutter.

"Ramallah?" he repeats as if astonished. *"Khalas. Ma feesh Ramallah. Kullha rahat,"* he says in broken Arabic. The words sound like they have been beaten up, bruised so blue they can hardly speak their meaning. But I gather them. "There is no Ramallah anymore," he says. "It all should be gone by now."

I search for the soldier's eyes, but his sunglasses are walls that keep me from seeing. I search for anything in his face to tell me more than the words he's just said about Ramallah. What does he mean? Are the homes all bulldozed down? And the people? My father and my family, will I find them? Will they wait for me? Fear is a blizzard inside me. A thousand questions clamor in my mind.

It was less than an hour ago that I took the bus from Ramallah to Birzeit. Now I am returning. How could everything disappear in less than one hour? Something must be wrong with me. Perhaps I do not know how to think, how to understand my world. Today I chose to sit up front when

I should have chosen to hide in the back. I should have known a front seat lets one see more of what lies ahead.

I want to open my mouth and let my feelings escape like birds, let them migrate forever. I am waiting for the soldier to step off the bus. But he doesn't.

He counts us, then takes out a radio and speaks. I don't understand, and I am somehow content that I do not. I do not want to know what he says about me or the bus, or what he plans to do.

He switches back to Arabic, takes the driver's ID, tells the driver to transport us all—the old passengers, the young, the mothers, students, everyone—to the Military Rule Center. He means the prison-court military compound on the way to Ramallah. I know where that is. It sits on the ground like a curse: large, grim, shrouded in mystery. In ten minutes our bus will be there.

New soldiers wait for us at the entrance to the compound. One walks to our driver's window, tells him to let all the passengers off, then turn around and leave. The driver apologizes to us. He says if it weren't for the order, he would wait for us no matter how long it took. I wonder if he is afraid to continue on to Ramallah, to be alone when he finds out whether it's really in ruins.

"Wait a moment," he says. "I will return your fare."

But no one can wait. "*Yallah! Yallah!*" a soldier goads. "Hurry!"

After a second head count, at gunpoint, we form a line and walk to a waiting area. We stand against a wall that faces the main door. The compound feels like the carcass of a giant animal that died a long time ago. Its exterior is drab, bonelike, and hostile.

We take out our IDs. Two soldiers collect them to determine if any of us had been caught in previous confrontations with the army. Our IDs inform on us. The orange-colored plastic covers, indicating that we all are Palestinian, pile up on the table like orange peels.

Two college students, with thick books in their hands, are quickly separated from the group. For a moment, my dream of going to college feels frightening.

"Hands up!" someone says, and one of the two soldiers now chooses the people he wants and inspects their bags, pockets, bodies. He skips the girls and women. All is quiet until he raises his hand to search a teenage boy standing next to me.

Even before the soldier touches him, the boy starts to giggle. The sound breaking the anxious silence is shocking. At first, the giggles are faint, then they grow so loud that soldiers from outside the yard hear and come to see. The boy's laughter is dry and trembling. Worried. I know what he feels. He wants to cry, but in spite of himself, in spite of the soldiers and the guns, all he can do is giggle.

Angered, the search soldier punches the boy, but like a broken cup that cannot hold its contents, the boy continues to laugh. The soldier punches him again. The boy's laughter now zigzags up and down like a mouse trying to flee and not knowing which way to turn. But a kick on the knee from the soldier's boot finally makes the boy cry. He folds down in pain and then is led inside the building.

We stand still like trees—no talking, no looking at one

another, no asking questions, no requesting water or trips to the bathroom, no sitting or squatting. We do not know what we are waiting for or why we are waiting.

The hours stretch like rubber bands that break and snap against our skins, measured by the ticking of boots, going and coming across the yard, in and out of the building.

I keep my eyes on our main guard, who now sits by the door. Lighting a cigarette from the dying ember of the one he has just finished and filling his chest with the flavor of fire, he makes frog cheeks and blows smoke rings that widen like binoculars as he glances at us through the smoky panel. He looks at us as though we are only suitcases in his custody.

I want to ask him if I can take out a pen and paper. If he lets me, I will empty myself of what I feel. I will distract myself from my hunger, for I have not eaten all day. And I will record details to give to my mother in order to avoid her wrath—if Ramallah is not really gone.

But something in my mind wags a warning finger not to ask, not to do the wrong thing. It's a finger like Mother's, telling me to get home in a hurry, not ever to be late. But I am already many hours late.

Mother tells me not to speak about politics. She is always afraid that something bad could happen suddenly. *"Khalas, insay, insay,"* she demands impatiently. "Forget, just forget." And I do. I know less about politics than do most of my classmates. I never even learned how the colors of the Palestinian flag are arranged. Sometimes I glance at the outlawed flag during street demonstrations. I see it for seconds only, before the hand that holds it is shot at by Israeli soldiers. At times, I see the flag drawn in graffiti on walls. Someone does it at night and leaves it for us to discover in the morning. The soldiers spray over it during the day. Anyone caught with the Palestinian flag is punished.

Mother does not want me or any of my siblings to do anything that could cause us even the slightest trouble with the army. *"Imshy el-hayt el-hayt wu qool yallah el steereh,"* she says. Walk by the wall. Do not draw attention to yourself. Be invisible if you can, is her guiding proverb.

If I see Mother again, I will tell her what happened to the bus at the checkpoint. "Why go to Birzeit?" She will slice at the air with her hands, half wanting to hear my answer, half wanting to hit me.

Birzeit is where students go to college after finishing high school in Ramallah. Some also come from Gaza, Nablus, and other cities, towns, and refugee camps. In Birzeit, many students become active in politics and have fights with the Israeli army. They chant on the streets that they want freedom from the occupation. But I did not go there to chant for freedom. I have my freedom. It is hidden in Post Office Box 34. This is what takes me from Ramallah to Birzeit.

Post Office Box 34 is the only place in the world that belongs to me. It belonged to my brother Basel first. He left Ramallah and did not want to give up the box, so he passed it on to me. On the days I don't go to Birzeit, I bury the key in the dirt under a lemon tree near our house. If I die, the key for the box will be under the ground with me.

Having this box is like having a country, the size of a

tiny square, all to myself. I love to go there, dig the key out of my pocket, turn its neck around, open the door, then slowly let my hand nestle in and linger, even if the box is empty. I wish I could open my postbox every day. I feel that my hand, when deep inside it, reaches out to anyone on the other side of the world who wants to be my friend.

Some postal worker in Birzeit must like me, perhaps because I put "Thank you to the postman" on all my envelopes. When many days go by without my coming for letters, I sometimes find a stick of chewing gum in my box. Someone has opened it first, written a line of cheerful poetry, then wrapped it again. Smiling, I skip out of the post office. I chew the line, taste its meaning. Paper and ink, poems and my postbox are medicines that heal the wounds of a life without freedom.

On some days, I wish I could stay inside my postbox, with a tiny pillow made from a stamp with a flower on it. At the end of the day, I could cover myself up with one pink-enveloped letter and sleep on a futonlike stack of letters from my pen pals:

Dimitri from Greece. He writes of a Greek holiday called No. I reply that all teenagers in the world should celebrate this day. Dimitri and I argue about baklava. He insists it's Greek. I assure him it is Arabic. Perhaps it is both, we finally decide to agree, since both our peoples love it.

Luis from Spain. He is unhappy for reasons I do not understand. His country is not occupied, and he does not have a strict mother like mine. But I like it that he always writes something about basketball. He says when he gets out on the court he forgets all his worries.

Hannah from Great Britain. What if I wrote "Great" next to "Ramallah" when I send my letter? From Great Ramallah to Great Britain. We would be equals then. Hannah's letters are always egg white, with the queen stamp, which I stare at for a long time. The crowned queen is beautiful. Hannah writes about the trips she takes with her family and the books she reads. She loves *Gulliver's Travels* and *Emil and the Detectives*, books that I, too, love, because Gulliver and Emil remind me of myself. Gulliver knows exactly what it is not to be free. And both Gulliver and Emil form fond friendships with strangers.

Sally, a grandmother from America, speaks about eating turkey on Thanksgiving. "Eating a country?" I write back. She explains. And I laugh because Mother dislikes the "Roman rooster," our name for turkey. She would never let one in our house, much less cook it for a celebration.

I have many pen pals: tourists, Holy Land pilgrims, and students who join pen pal programs to see the world through other people's words. Some write only once in a long while. Others write often. But all of them send me scraps of their lives translated into English, which I have been studying for six years, ever since I turned eleven.

In return, I tell my pen pals about my school, friends, teachers, studies. I describe the seasons, the land, the wheat and olive harvests, and the Eid celebrations. Looking into a hand mirror, I describe myself if I don't have a picture to send. Translating many words and sentences, I also write about the Arabic language. I explain that verbs in Arabic form roots that create trees of nouns and word structures. *An yaktub* means to write. *Maktoob* means a written letter. *Katebah* is a female writer. *Ala-katebah* is a typewriter. *Kitab* is a book. *Maktab* is a desk for writing. *Maktabah* is a library, the place where one finds books. All these words grow from the root verb *kataba*. Making words in Arabic is like planting a field with seeds, growing an orchard—words hang on the vines like grape clusters, leaves throw shadows of meanings to the ground.

I am eager to answer all my pen pals' questions about language. But when they ask me about my childhood, suddenly I have nothing to say. It's like a curtain comes down and hides my memories. I do not dare part it and look. So I skip all childhood questions and reply only about the day.

Today, I wish I could tell my pen pals that I was going to Birzeit to open my postbox, to meet their words. There were no letters from anyone. Maybe they were on their way, but the postal trucks were unable to get to Birzeit. The roads and mail system here are like our country, broken. Letters are like prayers; they take a long time to be answered. What would my pen pals say if I told them that I am standing at a detention center because I went to open my postbox for their letters?

Now, gazing at the ground under my feet, I remember that I need to make up something ingenious to convince Mother that I did not go to Birzeit to talk to college boys or do anything related to Palestine or politics. I usually cannot convince her of anything. She is cleverer than I am. She is cleverer than anyone I know. Perhaps ten mothers in Ramallah are not clever at all because she has gotten their share of cleverness.

When unsatisfied, she pokes my chest and curses me. To answer her, I write poems about the cruelty of mothers. "What difference is there between a mother and a soldier? None." I underline my answer. "Mothers and soldiers are enemies of freedom. I am doubly occupied."

I post the poems on the wall like freedom graffiti or tuck them in "her journal," a journal that I keep only for my mother. She reads it when I am gone.

Often, however, I write good words in her journal, hoping that when she sees them she will know that I care about her and be gentler with me. "God, I feel terrible for Mother because she works so hard. And I don't know what it is to be a mother in a land filled with soldiers and war. Please make her happy. Take from my happiness if that's the only way to help."

"Liar," she pencils next to my words, then erases it. The faint traces remain. I see them. We never speak about her journal, but we meet there to say the things we cannot say out loud.

My true journal is written with no pen or paper, but in my mind, with an invisible hand in the air. No one will ever find it. When Mother says to come home, I write in my mind that I feel at home nowhere. I want to wander the streets after school, walk forever, walk away from a world I do not understand, a world that tells me daily there is no place in it for me.

And it is not just Mother who is afraid and watches over me. Father does, too. My parents, Suleiman and Mirriam, whom I call Yaba and Yamma, often disagree on things, but when it comes to me, they act as though they never disagree. My father copies his feelings from Mother the way one copies homework. On some mornings, they whisper a few words, then my father pretends to go to work early. But he waits outside until I walk to school, and follows me.

He must want to see how I behave on the streets when I am alone. He does not know that I read him the way I read a street sign, and that I watch for him every day the way I watch for the snipers on top of the large buildings in Ramallah. They, too, watch how we walk and what we do. Without looking at them, we know exactly where they are. When my father walks behind me, as if he thinks he can outwit me, I feel sad. How little he knows me.

"Yaba, why not wait outside until I leave?" I said one morning.

"What for?" he asked.

"So that you can follow me," I fumed. He became outraged and charged after me. I bolted into a room and locked the door.

"Why do you challenge me?" he shouted. I opened the door and walked right up to him. He only shook his head, blamed my defiance on my schooling, and blamed himself for sending me to school.

"You dig your head into your *Nakleezi* books like a sheep, grazing all day," he said, and sighed, perhaps wishing he, too, could read English books.

I know that my father does not really want to put down my schooling, especially because of the way he treats the word *chair*, the only word in English he knows. He says it with pride, moves it around in his speech as though to gain a better view of things. He sits on it like it's a throne. Yet it is a lonely chair. My love for language and words seems to come between us. It takes away his authority over me. The books, not he, are my references.

The soldiers are another force that separates us. Father knows that they, not he, are the ones who control every one of us. We are not free to be a family the way he wants, with him a lion in our lives. He is like a lion in the zoo. Any of us can be taken away any day. No one can stop that, no matter how hard he roars from the fenced space allotted to him.

I compare my father with the fathers of other girls. He is poorer than many, and war lives inside him. Every night, he wakes up shouting that someone is going to kill him, kill us all. He punches at the air, kicks with his feet to free himself, and cries for someone to help him. Mother sleeps on the farthest edge of the bed to avoid getting hit. She pretends she does not hear his cries.

But every night I run to comfort him. I bring him a cup of water and sit beside him. I ask him to tell me what he sees. Catching his breath, he mixes words and tears. My father has no language for the pain and loneliness he feels. Is that because he has lived all his life not knowing freedom? Or does he hide his freedom somewhere, the way I hide mine in Post Office Box 34?

It is late afternoon, and we are still standing, still waiting at the detention center. My feet are aching for rest. Then, unexpectedly, I am released.

My tears drip onto my shoes. Tears are my secret ink, in

the absence of real ink. Liquid stories. On the air that comes into and leaves my chest, I write all the things that happen to me. "Now the soldier hands me my ID and tells me that I can go home . . ." I run toward the center of Ramallah, my heart heavy, as if it has stones in it. Questions rattle in my mind. What did the soldier on the bus mean?

But . . . Ramallah . . . is . . . still . . . there. *It is there.* Juabah newspaper shop, Salaam taxicab office, Fam boutique, Abu Azmi grocery shop, Zabaneh market, Salah pharmacy are all closed, but all are there. I want to hold Ramallah the way one holds oneself when there is no one else to touch.

Quickly, I realize that some fight between Palestinian protesters and Israeli soldiers must have taken place. The streets are deserted, except for speeding military vehicles. I walk cautiously. I feel afraid and alone. "Walk by the wall." Mother's proverb now guides me like a map. I hurry up until I get to the street near our home. But there, my heart begins to race, and my mind begins to fill with soldiers. Suddenly, I can see the kinds of things that my father describes in his nightmares. With every step I take, more images of war appear.

I stagger through the door under Mother's scrutinizing eyes. She is filled with fury. But one look into my face, and all turns into worry. "What happened?" she gasps.

I tell her that the soldiers detained me with many others. I tell her that, like Father, I have become ill with war. I describe to her the images I see. But I do not say I had gone to Birzeit. Perhaps she does not really want to know. For this, I am grateful.

"When a war ends, it does not go away," she says. "It hides inside us." She knows. "Do not walk that road," she warns me. "*Insay. Insay.*" "*Just forget!*"

But I do not want to do what Mother says. I cannot follow her advice. I want to remember.

> *Sinking in the sea*
> *Of forgetfulness*
> *I reach for the raft*
> *of remembering.*
>
> *Where the small girl*
> *I once was*
> *Stands alone,*
> *Holds a key*
> *to the postal box*
> *of memory,*
> *And awaits*
> *The day*
> *When she will*
> *Find her home*
> *By asking*
> *Her heart to*
> *Take her there.*
>
> *Listen.*
>
> *Today is that day.*

PART II

The Postal Box
of Memory
1967–1971

Written on my heart
All that I lost.

Shoelaces

The war came to us at sundown. Mother had just announced that our lentil-and-rice dinner would be ready as soon as Father arrived. She picked up Maha, my infant sister, held out a plump breast, and began to rock and feed her. I was three and a half years old but still wanted to be the one rocking in my mother's arms.

My two brothers, the noisy inseparables—Basel, six and a half, and Muhammad, a year younger—were chasing each other around Mother's summer garden. I stood at the door awaiting my father. Soon I would see him emerge from the curtain of evening shadows on the long gravel road that led to our home. As I did every evening, I was preparing to run toward him with all my might.

But because I owned one pair of shoes, and was allowed to wear them only on important occasions, I was barefoot.

When my father finally appeared in the distance, I hopped my way along the gravel toward him.

My dad was my favorite person in the world, and before the war I had an unwavering sense that all was well as long as he came home at the end of the day. Each time I met him, he embraced me with a splendid smile that made his right eye fade into the shape of a crescent moon. He reached out to me with his loofahlike hand, and I half hung in the air as I grasped two of his fingers and walked beside him.

My father often gave me five tries at guessing what treat he had in his pocket for us. When I could not guess by the fifth time, he gave me the first letter of the word, and then I guessed for certain. *M* for *mulabbas*, candy-coated almonds. *J* for *jawz hind*, coconut mounds. *K* for *kastana*, beetle-shaped chestnuts. *Q* for *qedameh*, salted and roasted chickpeas. *B* for *bizer*, roasted pumpkin, sunflower, and watermelon seeds, and *S* for *simsim*, sesame-seed bars, my favorite treat. I would break a bar into tiny bites to make it last for two days.

But on the evening of June 5, 1967, my father had no treats for us. On this evening he was the one rushing toward me, and soon I could see that his face had no smiles. Although he was saying something, it was only when he was closer that I could hear.

"Turn back!" he shouted. "Tell your mother the war has started," he ordered. "Run!"

I did not fully understand what he said, but every part of me felt the danger in his words. As I ran home, I fell on the gravel and scraped my knees, but I did not feel the pain—

except for a moment. I sensed that my father did not need to be bothered by a crying child.

Mother seemed to know exactly what my father's words meant. Her response astounded me. She struck her face with both her hands, dug her nails into her terror-stricken cheeks, and then she scratched. She said nothing, and her eyes gazed into the distance. It seemed like her soul had momentarily departed from our kitchen, where we all stood paralyzed.

Then my father rushed through the door, dropped the bags filled with food he was carrying, and turned to Mother. She shrieked with tears upon seeing him. But he spoke to her tenderly, in the same way that he spoke to me about the importance of closing my eyes and falling asleep when he blew out the kerosene lamp at night. He told Mother he had heard that Israeli warplanes had been targeting Palestinian homes and the safest thing would be to turn off all the lights, leave our house immediately, and sit in the water trench in the garden while we decided what to do. He also wanted to listen to the radio to find out which specific areas were being attacked, but the only radio we owned was a set the size of an oven, too big to carry into the trench.

Mother snatched Maha and held on to her tightly. Basel, Muhammad, and I held on to Mother's dress, and we all marched outside.

Inside the trench, I glued myself to my brothers, and my heart surrendered to the rhythm of our vigilant breaths, all rising and falling in anxious unison. With the tip of my head, I reached to touch my father's arm, which held us close. His other arm enclosed Mother. She was frantically trying to quiet Maha, whose siren cries threatened to draw fatal attention to our hiding place. Because there was no room for love and lullabies in the narrow trench, Mother snapped sharply at Maha, who quickly stopped her crying.

My parents exchanged anxious whispers. "Think with me," Mother urged. "What else should we do to be safer?"

"There is no escape from destiny," Father replied, his voice filled with pain.

I reached for him and held on to him firmly. I felt that something beyond what I'd learned or would ever understand was about to happen to us. My father would not be able to protect us. He could not make the war stop. He could not talk to the people in the planes and tell them that we had done nothing wrong.

As darkness enveloped us, I could not see the faces of my parents or my brothers. Then, suddenly, Mother whispered that she could hear footsteps. My father ordered us to freeze. I stopped myself from breathing.

We quickly realized the footsteps were those of a stream of people from neighboring villages fleeing their homes. Raising his voice just loud enough so they could hear him, Father asked what they knew. A man's voice answered. "After the planes attack, they will be combing the area house by house. Word is that they will butcher every living thing they find."

My parents exchanged a few words, then quickly agreed. It was time for us to leave. "Death in a group is mercy," Father said.

"First I must get into the house," Mother interrupted. "We need food for the children," she pressed. And she was right. Hunger was pecking inside my stomach like a bird.

"Then don't light even a match," my father cautioned her. And so Mother tucked my silent sister into his arms and set out for our house.

But before we could settle into the thought that food was within reach, a loud, pulsing noise sliced through the dark. Bullets were being fired at Mother!

"Yamma!" my brothers and I exploded. But our father shushed us into silence. Then the noise of planes filled the darkness everywhere. One plane seemed to be right above us, seeding the ground around us with bullets and bombs, and as it trailed off into the distance, it set nearby patches of the darkness afire. It was impossible to tell which side of the sky would be the next to blaze.

Dad flung himself out of the trench. He found Mother's foot and pulled her back to us. Frightened and confused, she searched herself for a fatal injury. "Suleiman," she begged my father, "I want to see my children one last time before I die." But the darkness surrounding us was merciless.

Father held Mother to his chest. "Mirriam, they missed," he whispered. Miraculously, she had escaped injury, and the warmth in Dad's voice allowed my blood to flow again through my veins.

Mother, shocked, had nothing to say. Then, suddenly, she demanded that we leave.

It seemed strange, but she picked up Maha and began walking toward the house. Basel, Muhammad, and I leapt after her as my father prayed hysterically that we come to no harm.

Inside the house, Mother snatched the pot of lentils and rice from the kitchen and wrapped it in a rag. Then she dashed into the darkness and searched for a bundle of golden bracelets that had been her dowry when she and my father married. I could hear her sigh of relief when she found them.

Mother then commanded that we put on our shoes. But I could not find mine, and the house was black as coal. "Yamma, where are my shoes?" I cried.

"Find them!" she ordered. My brothers and I obediently searched until all three of us found our shoes, then hurried outside.

Now my parents spoke urgently. My father said that if we didn't die that night, we'd have to sleep in the wilderness. We'd need clothes and blankets. When he came out of the house with a mound in his arms, he and Mother argued over whether or not to lock the door. They finally agreed: we would lock it and take the key with us.

People continued to pass by our house, spreading word of impending terror. A breathless man told my father that there was no one left in his village. He and the others were going to hide in the caves, then try to cross the bridge at the border to Jordan.

"Which caves?" Father asked.

"Just run with us," the man replied before disappearing into the darkness.

Father turned to Mother. "We must leave now," he said. His voice was sharp like a knife.

My brothers were ready. They held each other's hands tightly. Mother had secured Maha between her arms. My father strained to see the road from behind the mound of clothes and blankets he carried. But in spite of my desperate attempts to obey my parents' commands, my three-and-a-half-year-old hands were unable to lace up the one shoe I had put on. My right foot was still shoeless.

"Yamma, Yaba! Help me!" I cried in a hushed voice, lest I attract attention and we all die. But no one answered.

At that moment, a new wave of fleeing villagers rushed by. As they disappeared, everything faded into stillness. And my family was gone.

Had they just walked into the crowd and left me behind? Fear dug a hole in my heart. I could not grasp what had happened. I wanted to cry aloud, hurl their names across the darkness, but dread stifled my voice. I knew that the only hope for me was to instantly run in the same direction, leaving one shoe behind.

As I moved, sounds of distant gunshots and screeching swelled and then subsided. I kept running. When I looked behind, I could no longer see the giant shadow of our home. The world within and around me seemed to fade into the unknown. The gravel grated sharply into my skin. Once again, I commanded myself not to feel.

Soon, my ears detected voices. I waited cautiously, and when people approached, I attached myself to the end of their caravan.

Settling into the rhythm of this rapidly moving crowd, I could hear voices talking about a group of neighbors they expected to meet at the caves. The caves? My parents were heading toward caves! My heart filled with hope that my family would be there.

But my hopes disappeared when flare bombs lit up the darkness and formed a dome of light in the sky. Silhouettes of everyone suddenly became visible. Now the warplanes could locate us. Would real bombs follow?

Anticipating the moment of final destruction, people prayed aloud. They said that Allah is one. But as the lights and sounds of distant bombardment continued and no bombs fell directly on us, it became clear that neighboring areas were the immediate targets of attack.

We continued on, slowly sinking into a solemn calm. I saw that we were joining other clusters of people, as ghostly and stunned as we were. Among those ahead of us, I thought I saw my mother, her thick, dark braid waggling on her back.

Our group hurried to catch up to the group in front of us, and my numbed feet flew forward. The lights in the sky came and went, but I kept my eyes on the braid. I fell repeatedly, but quickly got up. My eyes never wavered. I was determined to reach my mother. I pushed myself closer and closer to where I thought I saw her until I was only a few steps behind her braid. When my fingers finally touched her dress, the war seemed to halt.

Thinking that I was with my mother again, I could see that I had lost the one unlaced shoe I'd had on. I began to feel the feverish fire in my feet. I let myself weep a little, hoping my mother would hear me, then I pulled on her dress and let it take my weight. The respite lasted for only seconds, however. As new flares flashed, a strange face turned to scold me. "Who are you?" she asked as she shook her dress free from my hand. Now I could see. The woman was not my mother.

In shocked disbelief, I dropped my hands to my sides, gripped my own dress, and could feel neither terror nor pain. My eyes searched for no one, and it barely mattered whether I walked alone or had people around. I could only put one foot in front of the other.

When we approached the area of the caves, I learned that there were many caves, in different places. Anxious voices pierced the air: should we hide or continue on? Some settled for hiding. But I found myself walking with those who chose to continue on until we arrived at the road that would lead to Jordan. It was deeply dark here, like everywhere else. So we waited for a long time for the night to be over.

When dawn finally lit up the world, I saw that I was surrounded by a large crowd. No one spoke to me, and I stared at the children who were clinging to their parents. I envied them having a hand to hold on to while I had none.

People were gazing into the sky as though a long line of unanswered prayers hung from it. They were cursing as they struggled to swallow their grief. They begged one another for a drink of water and begged God for mercy.

I wandered aimlessly, staring at strange face after strange face. And then, suddenly, I thought I saw my dad. "Yaba!" I called in a low voice, hoping it wasn't a mistake again. But he turned to me. Tears streamed down his face. Now I was certain.

Next to him stood Mother, holding my sister to her chest. My father and my brothers hurried to meet me, holding out their arms. Muhammad, the one who had first noticed that I was missing, offered me his shoes.

My heart ached, my feet burned, and something in me still felt confused and lost. But I was no longer alone. Once again, I was with my family. Together, we entered the second day of war.

Shelter

There were no cars or trucks on the Jordan road for as far as the eye could see. The June sun beat down fiercely on the tar, and on our faces. We stood for a long time before I asked if I could sit. My father insisted that I remain standing so that I could be ready to run. But I could no longer stand. My feet were bleeding and bruised, and thorns had broken under the skin. Each time I moved, it felt like I was stepping on needles.

Then, suddenly, it seemed as though my feet had disappeared from beneath me. And I fell to the ground, asleep. Frantically, Mother hovered over me while pressing Maha to her chest, and Basel and Muhammad shook me and pinched my cheeks until I woke up again.

"No one can carry you," my father explained urgently as he skinned off a piece of cucumber and rubbed it on my face. He offered me another piece to eat. At Mother's insistence last night he had brought the cucumber.

"Mirriam, do you really think it can replace water?" he had exclaimed in the darkness before we fled.

"I imagine so," she replied. *Imagine* was Mother's favorite word. In Arabic, she would say *batkhayyal*, which also means "to see the shadow of a thought," as if one is separated from it by a thin cloth. Mother seemed to dwell behind this veil, gaze through it, and long for uniting with its other side.

Now, standing only one step away from Mother, I could see that she had slipped behind that veil. Silently I begged her to come out and see me. But her gaze only floated far away to the horizon. When she finally spoke, the words were not directed at me.

"I hear something in the distance," she whispered, so as not to disturb the spider-thread perception connecting the sound to her ear, "perhaps an engine."

A fierce look came over my father's face. He closed his eyes, cupped his ears, and opened his mouth, as if to swallow the sound upon capturing it. He asked us all to listen; then he instructed that we hold hands and run behind him. "If it's a vehicle, I will stop it no matter what it takes," he vowed.

At the center of the road, he flung his arms open, ready to embrace a broad destiny. He implored the men standing by the roadside to join him. Many did, including a man who was carrying a gun. They huddled together, looking into one another's eyes to find courage, forming a human barrier, with terror the mortar that held them close. Everyone seemed to understand the strategy, and in no time other men formed new barriers along the road.

The noise now became increasingly loud, its diesel hum goading everyone's desperate hopes and deepest worries. People pushed one another in every direction as they fought to get closer to the road. My brothers and I planted our bodies where we could see our father, as if we were a compass needle and he was our North.

The source of the noise soon appeared as a white water tanker emerged from the silver spot on the horizon. People cried out to God in gratitude and jumped high in the air as if to deliver the words in person. But instead of slowing down, the tanker increased its speed as it approached the first group of men in its way. The men dashed to the side of the road at the last moment, and the tanker cut through them like a comb parting hair.

Then the water tanker approached Father and the barricade he had formed with the others. They raised their voices, promising that it would not pass through. They chanted that God is mightiest and asked for His help, which it seemed they would certainly need as it roared closer and closer. But then, when it was almost upon them, it screeched to a stop.

Quickly, people stuck themselves to the white truck like ants on an abandoned candy bar. Men climbed the giant balloon-shaped metal tank. Women, almost all of them carrying children, cried as it quickly became clear that the water tanker could transport only a small number of those waiting. The majority of families standing beside the road would be left behind.

Mother instructed my brothers and me to respond to all of her directions with the speed of a bullet. The three of us, who had become more like soldiers than children that day, nodded our heads in compliance.

Her directions were given upon hearing Father's voice, which came to us through the clash of many noises. But Mother seemed to understand every word. When he asked us to move closer, she commanded that my brothers climb up the tanker, find a way to fling their bodies on the windshield and block the driver's view. She then pulled me up by the arm and ordered that I squeeze myself among the bodies or, if I must, seep through them like water, but get myself to stand on the truck step, hold the door handle, and not let go. "Ibtisam, fight with everything in you," she roared.

I do not know how they did it, but Basel and Muhammad sliced through everybody until they ended up spread across the tanker's windshield. I took myself to the door handle. People pushed me away repeatedly, but I kept climbing until I had my hand on it. I pressed my face fiercely against the window and waited for Mother to reach me with her voice. When she called my name, I could see that she had been right behind me all the time and, to keep me on the step, had been supporting my weight with her body.

Looking inside, I saw the driver, his wife, and three children. They were piled up on one another, staring at all the mad faces that surrounded them. I could see my father's face pressed against the opposite window. He was unleashing a stream of curses, asking the driver to let us inside with his family, and to let as many people as possible hang on to the tanker for the journey to Jordan. Then pointing to a man who was aiming a gun at the truck's front tires, Father warned that if the driver did not consent, the man would shoot.

How could he open the door? the driver pleaded. People would force him and his family out, take the tanker, and leave. My father promised this would not happen. The driver hesitated—until we all heard the thundering of renewed bombardment.

Then the driver beckoned to his wife. The door opened a crack—and Mother, my brothers, and I instantly swirled around and shoved ourselves into the seat. The driver's wife, now with three children crying in her lap, looked into Mother's face and cursed. Trembling, she reached over to the door and locked it.

Reciting a short prayer, the driver pressed his hands against his face as though to comfort himself, then hit the horn until everyone in front of the truck moved aside. He announced that we would be moving nonstop until we reached Jordan. I did not know how long the drive to Jordan would take, but I hoped our time in the tanker would be short. My feet pulsed madly. As everyone pushed and tugged against one another, I ended up with my head pressed to the glass of the tiny window behind the seat.

My father was on the other side of the glass. But now he was holding a metal peg, which he used to knock on the water tank. He called to the driver that two knocks would be the signal to slow down so the men wouldn't fall off, and three knocks the signal to stop. The driver nodded.

The scattered sounds of bombardment made me jump each time I heard them. They also made the driver increase his speed. But whenever he did, Father slowed him down by knocking twice. Other men joined in, knocking twice with their hands to make sure the driver heard. The driver alternated his responses to them—first curses, then prayers for the time when he would be rid of us.

The men also burst into a clamor each time a plane zoomed above us. I could feel their voices washing over us like a giant wave that left me soaked in anxiety. But I kept my eyes on my father, who had become the solid center of my world.

The teeming tanker now rattled as it struggled to move as quickly as it could away from war. The driver reminded us over and over not to press too hard against the windows and doors. In no time Mother and the driver's wife, who said her name was Hamameh, began to speak as though they were friends. Hamameh invited Mother to visit her when the war was over and we all returned home. "Bring your children and come spend a day," she said.

Now, surrounded by the warm, womanly voices and calmed by the tanker's rocking motion, I fell asleep.

I jumped awake with the noises of many vehicles beeping, children crying, people shouting across a huge crowd, all swirled in dust and chaos. We were approaching the bridge over the Jordan River. Once we crossed it, we would be leaving the West Bank behind us.

Countless vehicles, bursting with people like ours, were trying to cross this bridge. Groups of fleeing people, carrying their belongings in knotted blankets, waited on the roadsides and begged for rides. Some walked in resignation or tried to wade through the shallow water under the trembling bridge.

Word was that there were shelters in Zarqa, Amman, Al-Salt, and other Jordanian cities. Many families were opening their homes to receive West Bank refugees. Mother and the driver's wife wept upon hearing this.

"There is still good in the world," Mother exclaimed.

"God does not forget anyone," Hamameh affirmed. It seemed that we were close to safety.

"We made it!" the driver announced the moment we crossed the bridge. He thanked God with a quick prayer. But even though we had entered Jordan, we could still hear warplanes right above us. Then they started to fire.

Our truck rocketed forward at a dizzying speed, as though fear were its only fuel. Other vehicles raced parallel to us and formed many lanes on the narrow paved road. A giant dust cloud quickly enveloped all the vehicles and made it impossible for us to see what was happening to those behind us. But I knew that my father and the men on the back of our truck were holding on to its bars as though their arms were made of steel.

It was afternoon when we arrived in Al-Salt City. At the

entrance of a shelter for women and children, Mother flung open the door of the truck and the nine of us, Hamameh and her three children, Mother and my sister, my brothers, and I, burst out, all sighing in relief. Our driver, Father, and the other men said they must leave us and go volunteer their help where it was needed. The driver asked his wife not to worry about him. And Father, who now sat beside the driver, told Mother he would come see us or find a way to send us word every chance he got. He held an arm out the window, and my brothers and I hung from it until the driver started up. Then we jumped off the truck step. But Father kept his arm out the window waving to us, and we waved back as long as we could—until the white water tanker finally disappeared into the distance.

Souma

The shelter was a three-story stone house. Before we entered, Mother said that she was unsure whether Maha was still breathing. "She's been silent for so long; I don't have the courage to find out if she's alive," Mother confessed. Without saying a word, Hamameh reached down to my sister's nose. She pinched and held it briefly. To our stunned surprise, Maha coughed and then cried.

We fought our way into the shelter, which wasn't much more than a box of strangers packed in like sardines. Every few minutes, sirens went off. *"Khatar, khatar,"* voices would shout. People would run up the stairs, then run down howling news about fires and bombings they'd seen from the second- and third-floor windows.

The sirens were warnings before or after bombardment,

and they were always followed by a silent moment of nause-ating anticipation of the destruction of our shelter. My brothers and my mother, Hamameh and her children all joined in the stair madness.

I hung on to my brothers and hopped along until I could no longer tolerate the pain of being elbowed or shoved or having someone step on my injured feet. The cuts I had from running barefoot had begun to swell, making it more and more difficult for me to walk.

I decided to sit in a corner of the basement. And there, standing almost invisibly in a cloud of dark and quietness, was a baby donkey. At first I could not believe my eyes. For one brief moment, the surprise made me forget everything else. I raised my arms and touched his face; he remained still. I spoke to him; he looked at me and listened. I knelt on the ground and pulled him toward me. He did not resist. I named him Souma and embraced him with my whole heart.

I stayed with Souma until the air raids subsided. But then the howling of stray dogs began. The war had awak-ened their pack instinct. They came to the city searching for food and corners to hide in. They sniffed, clawed, grunted, and yelped in frightening demon voices. Souma's ears stood like antennas measuring the danger. We were only one wooden door away from them.

"Be warned!" someone shouted outside. Expecting loud noises, I covered my head and plugged my ears with my fin-gers. But that did not keep me from hearing gunshots as bullets entered the bodies of the strays. An anxious cheer or two accompanied the shooting.

The packs retreated, but the injured dogs were left crying in voices that grew smaller and smaller until they resembled the whimpers of infants. Tears soaked my face. I knew that they were dying and that they had come to our door only because, like us, they were seeking refuge. But instead of understanding, we shot at them, the way the warplanes shot at us. I listened until there was only silence.

Crawling up the steps, I left Souma in the basement and went to be with the others. The women covered the windows with paper and cloth. They searched for charcoal but found none. Darkened windows would make it difficult for airplanes to notice light from our shelter and target it. The women then unfolded blankets that were stacked against the shelter wall like giant wafers. Children lay on them and formed tiny forts with covers that they drew over their heads. I lay down, too. I fell asleep, but my throbbing feet woke me up again and again. The women did not sleep. Instead, they passed the time by telling stories of the war in 1948, embroidering their memories with worry and tears. They only stopped when the call from the minaret of a nearby mosque announced the arrival of a new morning.

Allahu Akbar, God is greatest. Everyone awake repeated the words. But was God going to end the war today? End our flight and send us home? I wanted to know. We raised our arms above our heads in the shape of empty baskets for God to fill with the day's rations of our lives.

The women hoped the darkened windows would allow

the children who were still asleep to rest longer. But hunger awakened everyone. Food appeared and disappeared unexpectedly that day—mainly bread and tea were delivered to us when people outside remembered that we had nothing and knew no one around us. The following days were the same. We could never guess when or if we were going to get food.

Each time we did, however, the youngest and the sickest got their bread and tea first. Mother brought me my share and instructed that I eat every morsel. To check my temperature, she spread her hand on my forehead. She thought I had a fever, so she asked that I lay my cheek against the cool cement floor.

When I sat up and ate, Mother held my potato-size foot and measured its swollenness. I cried. She disliked my tears. "You will become blind and live in a corner forever if you keep on crying," she warned as she slammed her eyes shut for a moment to show me blindness.

I tested Mother's warnings. I clenched my eyes and attempted to see what she meant by becoming blind. But I discovered that, with my eyes closed, I saw more. I even saw things that were not around me—our home in Ramallah, the gravel road leading to it, the pine forest behind it, the green spearmint patches on the dry land, and the stone sculptures Father had taught us to build by stacking flat stones into human-looking shapes. He called each stack a *qantara*, but I called it a stone person. I now saw the *qantara* my father had once built to remind me that he loved me. And I saw the fig tree at the side of our house, alone in the field with one early ripe fruit hanging on a hidden branch. The sparrows had not gotten to it. The fruit hung like a kiss. Its neck was softly tearing. Soon it would be on the ground, sweet like nectar. The sparrows would feast on it.

With my eyes still shut, I saw my father appear before me, wearing his green shirt with the bulging chest pocket covering his heart. Inside it he kept his tiny black comb and scraps of paper with old and new lists of foods Mother had asked for, and a clip-on pen that poked out near the colorless button. In my mind, I ran and held his hand tightly. I did not want to let go of him. And, suddenly, I understood what Mother meant by the word *imagine*. I, too, could imagine. Blink. Blink. Blink. I could see anything I wanted to see, anytime I wanted. I needed no one's permission. And I could close my eyes and hide anywhere in my imagination, making the sounds of war more distant and less alarming.

In a short time, the shelter began to feel like a home, everyone in it belonging to one large family. Mother and Hamameh talked to each other all day long. My brothers spent their time playing with the crowd of shelter children. And Souma the donkey became my best friend; we were inseparable. The strangers of only days ago now remembered each other's names, the cities they had fled from, and directions to particular neighborhoods. They told of their pain and illnesses, and cried to one another whenever their stories felt too heavy to bear alone. They gave one another messages to pass on if the shelter was attacked and they died. Since no one knew how long the war would last, they decided that all would share the work and take turns sleeping. The women kept the shelter spotless, as if it were a home.

Our drinking water came from a rain well in the backyard and was stored in a clay urn. The urn had a thin base and could easily be pushed off balance, so only adults handled it. They watched over it carefully, snatching babies who crawled by it or shouting to warn children not to race near it. The urn had a mouth and two ears on its sides. An oversize tin saucer on the top looked like the rim of a man's hat, so the neck, round belly, and tiny base of the pot made it look like the only man among us.

Trash was left near the door in a rusted metal barrel. Stubborn flies quickly formed a lid for it until a group of boys rolled the barrel away and set fire to its contents.

The women who could do so nursed the infants of women whose milk had dried up. It was said, and repeated, that children nursed by the same woman would instantly become siblings and must never marry. Mother nursed only my sister, so we acquired no new siblings. But Mother gained a sister of her own—Hamameh, the driver's wife.

The two women agreed that if the war lasted a long time and their husbands did not return, they would help each other through whatever followed. But the war ended six days from the day it had started. For those of us at the shelter, it ended with two words, *Behawenha Allah*, spoken amid tears by an ailing man who leaned on a cane as he stood at the shelter's door.

All the faces cried, for *Behawenha Allah* meant "We have

lost so much that only God can ease our loss." Our loss? I knew that days ago I had lost my shoes and our home. But had everyone else also lost their shoes and their homes? I did not know why all the women, and especially Mother, who warned me often not to cry, were weeping uncontrollably now, tears streaming down their faces.

I, too, cried and held Souma close to me, because the words caused chaos in the shelter. Then everyone headed outside. I tried to go with them, but my feet, especially my right foot, made it impossible. The pain was too much for me, and I knew that, this time, if everyone left, I would not be able to run after them.

In the following days, everyone but Hamameh, her children, and my family left the shelter for good. Before departing, people shook their heads in sorrow and waved their arms as though to erase the memory of war. We, too, wanted to leave. We waited for Hamameh's husband and Father to come for us.

But no one came except a man and a woman whose wrinkled faces reminded me of my grandma. They were Um and Abu Muhammad, who had opened up their home to shelter us. They had spent the war days in Amman with their relatives, and now they had returned.

Um and Abu Muhammad were happy to see all of us who had taken refuge in their home. Though they had not met any of us before, they kissed our cheeks and held us for a long time while thanking Allah for our safety. Mother and Hamameh bent to kiss Um Muhammad's hand, but she pulled away, refusing any gestures of gratitude. "It's a duty," she insisted.

They invited us to stay in their home as long as we needed to, but Hamameh wanted to find her relatives in Amman. She asked Abu Muhammad if he knew them. He instantly recognized the names. Like Mother and Hamameh, who could recognize the names of many women, even if they were not actual friends, Abu Muhammad knew the names of many men. He sent word to let Hamameh's relatives know where she and her children were.

Within a day, a man in a taxi, stirring a cloud of dust as he pulled up at the door, asked for Hamameh. He was her uncle. The time for Hamameh and her children to leave the shelter had finally arrived.

There was nothing to pack. Hamameh turned to Mother to say goodbye. Suddenly, I was frightened. Was Father going to come for us? Would we know how to get back to Ramallah? Who was going to carry me? I stared at Mother, who silently leaned against the wall. But Hamameh understood her silence.

"Mirriam, my home is your home," she said to Mother. "Come with us until the men return." She tugged at Mother's shoulder.

Mother agreed. Um and Abu Muhammad said they would tell my father and Hamameh's husband where to find us. It was time for us to leave, too. "We're going," I cheered into Souma's big ear, thinking that he had no one in the world but me. I was ready to go anywhere as long as he came with me.

"We have no space in the car for a donkey," Mother snapped at me.

"I won't leave without him," I shouted. "Yamma, let him come with us," I begged. I gripped Souma with all my might as Mother tried to peel me away from him.

Um Muhammad came between us. She quietly said that Souma belonged to her.

"No! He belongs to me," I protested.

"But he would be so sad to lose his home," she said.

Now I could see what she meant. And so I let him go.

Hospital

Hamameh's new home was one room and a kitchen. She gave us a mattress and the kitchen space to sleep in at night. During the day, she and Mother worked in the house and talked. I silently awaited my father.

Finally, when the moon was full like a cantaloupe, he and Hamameh's husband appeared. Although the war had ended, they said we were not free to go back to the West Bank. My father also announced that he had found work transporting soda pop from a factory to local shops. We cheered. Soda pop, especially orange flavored, was a great treat.

In the morning, my father let Basel and Muhammad and me ride in the pickup truck he drove. It was filled with soda bottles evenly arranged in crates like egg cartons. The glass bottles made a jingling sound. Abu Omar, owner of the truck, had offered Father a tiny room to sleep in until he found a new place for all of us.

My dad had also bargained for a daily bottle of pop for each of us as part of his pay. My heart overflowed with love for him. He never forgot about treats, though now I could no longer run to greet him, for my right foot had ballooned and become purple and shiny like an eggplant. Alarmed, my dad said he would take me to the nearest hospital. The next day, as soon as he finished his deliveries, we all went.

The hospital was the largest building I had ever seen. It looked like a giant matchbox. In the distance, spruce trees stood straight like candles surrounding it. Vehicles lined the parking lot outside, and crossed iron bars secured the windows.

On the inside, sharp smells—vinegar, alcohol, purple liquid iodine, red Mercurochrome solution, and soap—filled the air. Cotton and needles in steel trays rattled on carts that busy nurses pushed before them.

Doors snapped opened and shut. Many people walked out as others entered, some leaning on wooden sticks or on the arms of family members. Those who sat waiting cradled their pained faces with their hands.

The color white was everywhere, and it mixed with the cold smells and the fog of fear that hung in the corridors. Squirming in Father's arms, I cried that I wanted to go home. But he begged me to let a doctor examine my foot, promising me a giant piece of sesame candy if I did.

Before I replied, a male nurse with a thick mustache and a warm voice like my father's came to see us. My parents explained to him what had happened to my foot. Nodding, the nurse led us into a room where a doctor soon joined us.

The doctor cradled my foot. He raised and lowered it, twisted it right and left as though it were his, smiling all the while even as I cried.

"Had you waited any longer, this foot would have been damaged permanently," he said. Mother began to explain that we were in a shelter, that she had been unable to do anything. The doctor reassured her that he himself was a refugee and understood the plight of parents during war.

I was to stay a night at the hospital for initial treatment and supervision. My parents promised they wouldn't leave me, while my brothers inched closer, determined to spend the night with me wherever I was going to be.

The doctor disappeared behind a curtain as we spoke. When he returned, he hid one hand behind his back. He then turned me on my side, and an injection took away my awareness of all that followed.

The next day, I woke up in an enormous room full of strangers. All in beds. Some lay under spiderwebs of white cloth that suspended their arms or legs. Some had their heads bandaged. The eyes of those who were awake stared listlessly into space.

I felt the blankness of the hospital sheets spread over me, covering my world with white. My parents had promised not to leave me. Why weren't they here?

I moved my body, but one of my legs was bandaged so stiffly it made me lose my balance if I tried to sit. I screamed and flailed my arms in outrage and frustration, hitting the bed beside me. Dozens of eyes turned to look at me. The doctor I knew came running to assure me that my parents would return at the end of the day. I waited.

My father, Basel, and Muhammad did come, my dad holding out a giant bar of sesame candy. He said getting the candy was the reason they had left. That made me happy. And the doctor said my foot would soon improve. He handed Father a sack of tablets, bottles, and ointments. We were to go home but would have to come back several times for follow-ups.

"Where is Mother?" I asked. I wanted her to be at the hospital, too. My father understood my disappointment. "We'll be home in no time; she's waiting for you," he assured me, and he tickled my cheek until I smiled. But I worried that Mother did not want to see me as much as I wanted to see her. There was only one mother in our house, and all of us wanted to be with her all the time. But she had four of us. Perhaps seeing any of us would do for her. Now she was with my sister. My dad, however, was different. With him I felt important, loved just for being myself.

Later, back in Hamameh's kitchen, when it was time for Father to drive to Abu Omar's house for the night, I clung to him and would not let go. He tried to pry my hands off, but I exploded in such distress that he had to stay by my side. Finally, he left me, ran out, and began to drive off. But Basel and Muhammad, wanting to help me, followed so close to the wheels that he stopped and turned around, the headlights circling the inside walls of the kitchen.

When my dad returned to hold me, his eyes filled with

tears. "I feel so torn," he said. Then he decided: he would take me with him. I joined him in the truck and looked back with thanks at my brothers, who leaned against the door, smiling at our victory.

The room where my father and I slept at Abu Omar's was at the edge of a garden that surrounded a stone villa. We unlatched the gate. The garden was filled with plum, lemon, and fig trees, and had a row of jasmine, rose, and hibiscus bushes. The hibiscus blossoms rolled themselves like cigarettes when they went to sleep. But the jasmine could never sleep. Its star flowers were forever wide-open, giddy with fragrance.

A narrow bed, a wooden table, and a kerosene lamp awaited us. Everything was quiet. My father warned that any noise could wake up Abu Omar and make him angry; then Dad might lose his job and there would be no more of the soda he brought home every day. I nodded in silence, avoiding even a whisper.

In the morning, Abu Omar and his three grown daughters greeted us. He and my father talked about the day's work while the daughters left to make tea and a breakfast of fried eggs, sour yogurt, apricot jam, and sesame butter.

The three daughters reminded me of Mother when she was happy. They had long, dark braids ending with colorful ribbons. They spoke softly and, when giggling, hid their teeth with their hands. They took turns gesturing toward me, encouraging me to join them. Alarmed, I shook my head. They ignored that. To tempt me further, they brought out a box of candy. But I felt they were insisting too much on separating me from my dad. I got mad at them.

When breakfast arrived, I was too anxious to eat or hold on to anything other than my dad. It became clear that I would not let go of him. So Father assured Abu Omar that my presence wouldn't distract him from the day's work.

But the daughters would not give up coaxing me to remain with them. They brought a cloth sack filled with toys, whistles, and balls, and poured it out before me. "Choose the ones you like," they offered.

I only wanted my dad, who was now rising from his seat, heading to a sink to wash his hands. I thought he was leaving. Worry welled up inside me like a wave. Unable to stand, I threw myself onto the floor behind him. I wrapped my arms around his feet and cried inconsolably. At last the girls seemed to understand. They returned the toys to the cloth sack and handed it to my father. "For her," they said. But I did not want toys.

I spent days and nights glued to my dad. The shopkeepers where we delivered the soda began to expect to see me. After pulling the crates into their shops, they poked their heads inside the truck window and asked me about my foot. They tossed mounds of candy in my lap that I chewed for hours. But I always kept some of it for my brothers.

My foot finally healed, and feeling stronger, I no longer insisted on being with my father all the time. Soon my parents bought me a pair of chocolate-brown boots. I could wear them whenever I wanted, not only for important occa-

sions. Basel and Muhammad taught me how to lace and un-
lace them, and I practiced and practiced until I could do it
easily.

Now I walked again, ran and played in the streets like a
monkey. On the final follow-up at the hospital, the doctor
smiled as though it were his own foot that had healed. "We
won the battle," he said, shaking my foot affectionately, the
way one shakes the hand of a friend.

Lentils

Hamameh's children, my brothers, children from dozens of other homes, and I played along a street that split our neighborhood like a spine. As we crossed back and forth, the cars slowed down. But one day, a car nearly struck a boy. He was not injured, but his legs shook under him like leaves in the wind. With his face pale as a lemon, he lay on the street, crying. He said no each time the driver tried to lift him.

Then the boy's mother came, hurtling toward us, not knowing whether her child was alive or dead. She was a frenzy of fear. We looked on as she pounded the driver's chest. The man took the blows and remained silent as a stone. Seeing his mother's grief, the boy willed himself to get up. He wiped his tears on his sleeve and said that he was fine. He wanted to play again. But his mother pushed him in front of her, and they both walked home. One moment the woman thanked God for his safety, the next she cursed and wished the boy dead.

Hearing about this incident, Mother became apprehensive. She couldn't keep us indoors, nor could she make certain we would be safe outside. When Father arrived that evening, she had made up her mind. One month in Hamameh's kitchen was enough. We had to move.

Gazing at each of us for a moment, Father said he, too, was worried for us. But he had not earned enough money to move us out of Hamameh's kitchen. And there were few homes available. The city of Amman was flooded with refugees like us who had fled during the war and could not return to their homes.

Mother said she had heard that, after the war, the government of Jordan had turned many schools into temporary housing for West Bank refugees. The students would not return till September. So she insisted that we move to a school. We would have playgrounds, and she would not be preoccupied with our safety, she argued. Father agreed.

The next day, Mother and Hamameh talked about our leaving. "Perhaps it won't be long before we see Ramallah again," Mother said. "Suleiman has already registered our family with the International Red Cross." She raised up her hands in the gesture of a prayer. "The names of those who are granted permits will be announced on the radio. I will keep the radio on all day."

"But all the cities are occupied now. Don't you know what that means?" Hamameh protested. She bit her anxious lips between the words. "Will it ever be safe to go back?"

Mother seemed troubled. But she was certain about one thing: we would return to Ramallah no matter how long the wait.

Now the war sisters held each other's faces; they would never forget. In silence deep as the sea of their sorrow, they kissed twice on the cheeks, then parted.

And so we moved to the school. Mother said she missed talking with Hamameh. She wanted to see her. But I felt that even if she never saw her again, Hamameh's name, like its Arabic meaning, "dove," would always fly, glowing across the sky of Mother's memories, leaving feather prints of a kindness birthed from the cruelty of war.

The school playground was filled with boys who kicked balls hard, tackled and punched one another, and fought as though they themselves were engaged in war. They broke many windows. Nothing got fixed. Day and night, the hot air streamed in and out of the brokenness. I lay inside on the tile floor and cooled my skin.

While my brothers played with the boys, I explored the classroom that had become our home. A band of children joined me. The shelves had been emptied before we arrived, the chairs and tables pushed to the edges of the room to create space for sleeping. Blankets were heaped in a corner. Shoes piled up by the door like beetles. People mostly walked barefoot in the building. A blackboard covered the front wall from one end to the other.

I wanted the chalk resting on the board's edge. Other children wanted the chalk, too. We all jumped up, gripped the board's edge, and hung from it trying to reach the chalk above us. The board shook. We ran away quickly and squatted in the farthest corner of the room as the board tore off the wall and fell.

The noise brought Mother and the other women running. They set the board upright against the wall, but kept it on the ground. Children then flew to the chalk sticks like bees to flowers. Hands reached over heads as everyone wanted to draw something. When Mother saw me scribbling with all my energy, she drew the first letter of the Arabic alphabet. "His name is Alef," she instructed, returning the chalk to my hand. She asked me to draw him.

Alef was a long line that stood vertically and ended with a round circle. It looked like a Popsicle, a dandelion, a sunflower, a streetlamp, or a man with a hat on his head, like my dad in winter. I thought Alef lived inside chalk sticks. Because I wanted to be friends with Alef, I took a piece of chalk with me wherever I went.

In no time, I loved Alef with all my heart and also blamed him for anything I did not like or understand. When I wet my bed at night, I blamed him for not waking me up. When I dropped my plate, scattering food everywhere, it was Alef who had tripped me. When I got mad at Alef, I drew him on the board and left him there screaming for me to forgive him and come back. He put his fingers across his lips, indicating that he wouldn't do again whatever he'd done. I left him but quickly returned. I could not stay away from Alef long, but he did not know that.

I introduced Alef to my father when he came to see us after days of absence. At Mother's urging, Father had taken additional work at night to save up money. He had also found a new home for us in an area called Marka. That very day we left the school. But unlike the baby donkey, Souma, whom I loved but had never seen after we left the shelter, Alef, my chalk pet, could come with me—tucked into my pocket.

A man in a red-and-white headdress met us outside our new home. He led us in and gave us the key. Mother smiled at Father, who in turn reminded the man that, if we were allowed to return to Ramallah, we would leave with only a day's notice. The man agreed.

Our new home was only a single room. Mother set up a kitchen in one corner and marked it with my chalk. We were to stay out of the kitchen.

The paint on the walls and ceiling was peeling, paint chips tumbling to the floor like dried-up petals, resembling the leaves falling from the September trees outside. I helped Mother by collecting the paint flakes, keeping them in my pockets, then tossing them to the wind.

Our room's window overlooked the shops at the center of Marka. We watched people come and go. In only a few days we could recognize the recurring faces. The coffee shop, with its two tiny tables and many chairs, drew the men who played card games, chess, and backgammon, and threw dice. When their games were done, they leaned back and smoked water pipes called nargilehs.

They breathed in and out of the long pipes that came out of bubble-filled glass jars sitting on the ground before them. The pipes were decorated with gold, red, yellow, and green threads and beaded like holiday clothes. We stuck straws in water cups to imitate water-pipe smoking. But Father chastised us. He did not want us ever to smoke.

The grocery store that shared a wall with the coffee shop was too packed for any shopper to enter. Cases of lentils, chickpeas, rice, beans, and dried foods obstructed the entrance. Shoppers stood outside and asked for what they needed. Two balanced brass plates made up the scales. Iron pieces a kilogram or half a kilogram on one plate indicated the weight of the food on the other.

We purchased flour from this store. But when we opened the sack, a gray mouse ran out of it. The shopkeeper said he could not guarantee the absence of mice. We kept the flour.

Early mornings, Mother prepared the dough for our bread. She sifted flour, mixed it with water, salt, and yeast, and pounded it together. When she let it rest, we would poke our fingers into the dough to draw faces. Father then took the flat loaves to be baked in the community oven. But the bread he brought home had none of the faces we'd drawn. I wondered what had happened to them.

Daily we ate lentils, the only meal we could afford. My brothers and I hated lentils. They sat on our aluminum plates like mouse eyes, and we wished they would scamper off like the mouse that ran out of the flour sack.

Mother warned of illnesses that befell children who did not eat their lentils and of ghosts that stalked them in their sleep. But we could swallow the fear of ghosts more readily than we could swallow the spoonfuls of lentils. When we resisted, she forced our mouths wide open and poured the lentils in. They tasted like medicine. They made us want to throw up. But if we did, Mother hit us for having wasted the only food we had and for dirtying our clothes.

Mother washed our clothes mainly on Fridays, when Father had no work and could drive us to a stream where many people gathered. My brothers and I rode in the back of the truck screaming into the wind and laughing wildly. At the top of our lungs we would yell all the expressions Mother had told us we should never say because they were impolite. Then we made up songs in which the forbidden words were repeated over and over, until we arrived at the stream.

There, Mother met other women. Squatting or kneeling beside large piles of laundry, they used stones to rub the clothes clean. Then they built fires. In large tin cans they boiled the white pieces with a powder called Neeleh because it turned water blue like Al-Neel, the Nile River. The bubbles in the washtubs rivaled the bubbles in the water pipes smoked by men at the coffee shop.

While the women did the wash, my father and the other men, hoping to provide the meal for the day, hunted for porcupines in the areas surrounding the stream. My brothers played with marbles or chased a soccer ball with other boys. I raced against children my age, but mostly I watched my brothers play.

We were to stay away from the water. A month earlier, a boy had drowned. The water stole him, then dragged his body far away before it left him on a bank downstream.

"Two things should never be trusted—water and

snakes." This warning spread along with the story. And the stream seemed to slither like a watery snake. Was water an animal? Was it alive? It ran much faster than I could. Water was a puzzle that scared and excited me. I liked it and looked forward to seeing it every week. But then, without any warning, our Friday visits to the stream came to a stop.

It happened on a typical Friday morning, when a much older boy, thinking no one was watching, took Basel's hand and pulled him away from the crowd. I looked up and saw them walking toward the road.

I shook Mother's shoulder. "Yamma, someone is stealing Basel," I said, pointing to where the two boys were about to disappear. Mother screamed, and a crowd ran to the rescue.

The boy, Zazi, was known for harming younger children. Zazi's father beat him in front of all of us, spit in his face, and begged for forgiveness from my father.

But after that morning, my parents decided to leave us at home when they went to do the wash. They took my baby sister, Maha, but locked me and my brothers up in the house. We watched the world from our window and waited. We ached with longing for the only joys we'd had—running freely, being outside, and getting lost in games that made us briefly forget war, fear, and even lentils.

To cheer us up, Father brought back an extra barrel of water. Mother mixed soap in it to create bubbles. Then she poured it on the floor, took off our clothes, and let us play naked for hours. We threw our bodies on the slippery tiles, gliding fast until we hit the wall. I wished I could glide right through that wall—all the way back to our Ramallah home.

Pastries

Maha became ill. She wailed and would not nurse or sleep. Mother said she was going to take her to Um Ahmad, a neighbor who would give her an herbal remedy. Um Ahmad remembered ailments and their herbal cures the way one remembers names of friends or family members.

Bundling my sister in her arms, Mother said that my brothers and I could play in front of the house. As always, even though I was younger than my brothers, she instructed me to keep an eye on them and run and get her in case of trouble.

I sat at the doorstep thinking of Alef, who had disappeared when the last piece of chalk grew short, then crumbled into nothing between my fingers. Like me, he moves from home to home, I thought. I missed Alef and the white dust he shed, like a pet, each time I ran my hand on him. Missing Alef made me miss the baby donkey, Souma, too. I felt Souma was gone forever. But Alef? Far away in my heart I knew that someday I would go to school, find a blackboard, hold a stick of chalk with my fingers, and once again draw him. He would wake up and yawn. He would jump to meet me and would once again live in my pocket and help me do all kinds of things.

My sister's loud cries coming from Um Ahmad's house interrupted my thoughts. But there was nothing to do. I busied myself by studying the shadows on the ground, the corners of buildings, and how, as people crossed the court-yard, their shadows imitated everything they did, just as younger children imitated older ones.

The shadows, I could see, were mixtures of colors— blue, purple, gray, and perhaps an unlit red that got sifted out at the end of the day to give the night its darkness. I fol-lowed the shadows of my brothers, who always locked arms as they walked. Then the shadow of a wheeled wooden cart appeared.

The man who pushed it had just pulled out a large tray of hot pastries from the bakery. The aroma of sweet syrup on baked goods filled the air. I felt dizzy with a sudden hunger as my brothers and I cut through the courtyard, ex-changing glances that confirmed we could read one an-other's minds. We had not eaten pastries in a long time.

"This tray holds baked-to-golden-perfection *basbooseh*," the man trumpeted. I knew the taste of *basbooseh* and loved it. Before the war, Mother had made this treat by mixing semolina flour, yogurt, and sugar. She topped the mix with slivered almonds and baked it. When it was done, she drenched it with sweet syrup.

"Sweeten your mouth!" the man encouraged. I sighed. My chest rose and fell with his words; my eyes dug like spoons into the pastries. But I pushed my hands into my pockets, kept my hunger tucked under my skin. Basel and Muhammad stood on the other side of the courtyard. They too had their hands in their pockets. It seemed to me that while we were three children, we had the same feelings, as though we were one.

A woman called out that she wanted pastries. Leaning out from a window, she threw coins wrapped in cloth to the courtyard. The pastry man caught the money and hurried to deliver the sweets.

At that moment, my brothers swept to the cart with astonishing speed, clutched its big handles, threw their bodies against it, and wheeled it toward our home while I watched astounded. The cart was twice their size. The instant they reached the door, I jumped up and held it wide open for them. They slid the tray off the cart, carried it to the center of our room, and locked the door behind us.

Without tasting, chewing, or saying a word, we ate one piece after another, stopping only to take in giant breaths, until nothing was left on the tray except our sticky fingers spread anxiously on the metal. Then we leaned against the wall, our bellies distended before us, and awaited the unknown.

Fists pounded at the door, but we had become lost, entranced by what we had done. The pastry man threatened to break down the door. We jumped closer to one another. Then his voice mixed with the voices of other people. Mother's and Um Ahmad's voices now joined in. "I'll protect this door with my body," Mother shouted. My sister's cries, amid the clashing voices, rose like a siren.

"Open the door!" The command bellowed from every direction. Hands climbed up on the window bars.

"Don't eat more than a piece," she shouted. "Open the door," she now begged, her voice sticky like our hands. "Open the door," men yelled out. The men at the door were frightening us. I wanted my dad.

Then the words of the man who had rented us the room rose above all the voices. "I have a key," he thundered. We hid the tray behind us as the door swung open, and we watched in shock as the pastry man staggered in, drunk with anger. He wanted to see how many pastries were left. When he saw the empty tray, he looked around to see if we had emptied it into another container. When he realized that we had eaten every single piece, he stomped his feet like a beast. Charging toward us, he grunted that he was going to eat us alive, just the way we ate his pastries.

The crowd restrained him. Someone reminded him that we were hungry refugees and were to be pitied. "God shall compensate you," another affirmed.

Now the pastry man covered his face with his hands and moaned that his own children were waiting to be fed. "*Allah Be'awwed*," everyone said, trying to console him. "Allah shall compensate you." Then the shopkeepers dipped their hands into their own pockets. They donated money for a dozen pieces. "But you owe me for the entire tray," the pastry man told Mother before storming away.

Now, after thanking the men and shutting the door behind her, Mother was overcome by worry that quickly turned into rage. She turned to us. "Where will we get the money?" she exploded. "Where?" She pinched our skin into pain buttons and twisted my ears till they turned hot like embers.

When my father came home, he too took a turn at hitting us. "We are only guests in Jordan," he bellowed. "Stealing is not what a guest should do. We will be thrown out on the street if you ever behave like this again." The blows of his belt left long, dark stripes on our backs. We named those striped bruises *shawarea*, streets. For many days, up and down those streets, our pain tingled like unrelenting rows of ants.

My parents imposed a tight curfew on us. We were not to set foot outside the door. "For three months," Father seethed. But Mother shortened the punishment to one month, reminding him that he was not the one who had to stay in the house all day with us.

Grateful, we wanted to embrace her. She flicked us off in agitation. But our sentence of confinement was suddenly forgotten when the tiny people I thought lived inside the radio set announced a list of names approved for return to Ramallah. Our family's was included.

"Did you hear that?" Mother shouted as she raced to the radio, turning the volume up. We had. We danced and clapped to her happiness. Our family's name was repeated again within an hour. And that night when Father arrived home we quickly ate our lentils. The key to our Ramallah home dangled from Mother's chest, beating out a rhythm along with her laughter.

Neighbors came to say goodbye. They had tears in their eyes and concern for us. But we did not dwell on the possible dangers. After living for two weeks in a shelter, a month in Hamameh's kitchen, a month in a classroom, then two months in Marka, what mattered most was how homesick we felt.

The pastry man also came. He forgave us. "We lost Palestine," he said. "The pastries are nothing." Then he flung his arms wide as though to throw away any crumbs of a grudge he had held against us.

Return

We drove to the bridge that divided the east bank of the Jordan River from its west bank, where hills and valleys curved like the laps of a thousand mothers. Images of Ramallah filled my mind. And I wanted to know—would Ramallah be the same? And would we really be allowed to return?

We had heard that some men were asked to turn back at the bridge; their families were torn apart as the women and children were allowed to cross over to their cities but the men could not. When we arrived at the bridge, throngs of refugees were waiting to learn their fate. My father went to the area where the men were instructed to go. International Red Cross workers gave us blankets and cans of Spam and sardines. The tiny dead fish inside the sardine cans seemed to be lying helpless, waiting for something, just as we were.

My brothers and I were too worried to eat. We waited at the bridge for two days and kept looking in the direction where our dad had disappeared. We even refused the big chocolate bars a Red Cross worker secretly handed us after Mother told her that we had not eaten since we had arrived.

The hours of waiting piled up like the flies that buzzed in the camp. Then someone shouted out a list of names that included ours. "And take off your shoes, for all shoes must be inspected," the voice added. Barefoot and trembling, I stuck close to Mother. After a long wait, a man brought back a giant cart of mixed-up shoes and tossed them toward us. Everyone dove in to sort through the pile and find his own pair. I threw myself at mine and quickly put them on. When no shoes were left, the moment for us to cross the bridge finally arrived, and together my mother, brothers, sister, and I crossed over.

We had been told not to wait for my father because it took longer to question the men. I wanted to wait for him no matter how long it took. But now that we had crossed the bridge, we were not allowed to cross back. I worried that he might be kept in Jordan. I tugged at Mother for answers. But she had none.

On the other side of the bridge, Red Cross workers, wearing porcelain-smooth white helmets with red lines on them, looked like police as they offered us candy and said, "Welcome." We walked past them silently, gazing at the older people who had crossed the bridge before us and now knelt and kissed the dust as though it were the cheek of someone they loved. Then we walked to where lines of noisy buses in dust and smoke clouds awaited us.

Drivers called out the names of many destination cities. We listened and waited. And when we heard someone call "Jerusalem-Ramallah," my brothers and I charged onto the bus. We hurried to the backseat and stuck our faces against the glass, hoping to see across the bridge to where our father was. But the other side of the bridge had become hidden from us. Now we were in one country, our dad in another.

The ride felt long, and the belly of the old bus growled and sputtered on the winding roads until we arrived in Jerusalem. We took a second bus to Ramallah. A third took us to the edge of the gravel road where every day I had waited for my father to return home from work.

Now we would discover the answer to our most dreaded question: Had our house been destroyed? At first, we hesitated. We said the prayer of the desperate, *"Ya rab!"* asking God that He might be kind to our hopes. Then we raced toward the answer until it was before us. There, bathed in the setting October sun, was our house. Still standing.

We dropped everything and rushed up to it. We touched it. We kissed the stones and threw open our arms and pressed our chests and cheeks to it. We were home.

In the front yard, near the trench where we had hidden on the first day of the war, Mother picked up a large bullet, one that she believed had been aimed at her. And on the step in front of the green door, I found the shoe I had not been able to put on. It had been lying there, waiting for me, for four months and thirteen days.

We walked around our house. Our summer garden had mostly dried up and died. Only the *nana*, spearmint, had survived. The birds had hollowed the tomatoes into shells. Ants trafficked in and out of the eggplants. The earth was dry and broken. The roofless room Father had built for water storage was open, its zinc sheet cover lying on the ground and the ladder thrown near it. The water supply had almost completely disappeared; what was left was covered with dust and dirt.

The shutters and front window were open. Beyond the iron window bars, everything inside was quiet. A bird fluttered through the bars and flew out. We wondered whether snakes and scorpions had also nested in our belongings.

Stuttering the name of God, Mother walked to the green iron door, its two sides sealed at the center with a large locked bolt. She pushed the key into it and pressed. But the key did not move, and when she tried to pull it out, she could not. The key was stuck. "The lock needs to be oiled," she muttered. Where would she find oil?

Our house stood on top of a hill. On three sides there was nothing. On the fourth lived the Mahasreh, a cluster of related families who had moved to Ramallah upon the takeover of their town, Beit Mahseer, in the war of 1948. They were aloof and kept to themselves.

The Mahasreh house closest to us was half a mile away. We could not see the rest of their dwellings from where we stood because they lined the stretch of road that connected our house to the Ramallah-Nablus road. To reach the road, we always cut through the Mahasreh area going and coming, and that annoyed them. They accused us of picking cherries, grapes, or figs from the trees and vines in their yards. We dreaded asking the Mahasreh for anything. But tonight, our only hope was to knock at one of their doors.

And although they did not say they were happy to see us again, they gave us a bottle cap filled with olive oil. Mother was grateful.

She put the oil on the key and waited till it slowly spread inside the bolt. Then she tried to turn the key—and this time it moved. She gave the two sides of the door a big push, and they flew wide open like welcoming arms.

Things in our house seemed to be exactly the way we had left them. To the right, the brown sewing machine was still nestled in one corner, the green bed in another. The red-and-yellow straw carpet covered the center of the room, and the honey-colored Formica cupboard divided the space into a living room and kitchen. But when Mother lifted the sky-blue thermos that sat on the tiny kitchen table, she gasped. She pointed to a hole that a bullet had torn in its base. The hole was large enough to stick my finger inside. "Someone shot into our house through the window," Mother announced. Suddenly, our home no longer felt safe.

And the thermos was dear to Mother. She had bought it with money she earned from months of sewing. It had helped her save on kerosene by keeping water hot so she did not have to boil more water every time she needed to mix it with milk powder. The bullet had entered the base of the thermos, left it, and settled inside the kitchen wall.

Mother took the thermos and went outside. We leapt after her and watched as she dipped cupfuls of filthy water into the thermos. Had the glass lining been ruined? We held our breaths as we waited for water drops to fall. But the thermos did not leak. It held water the way a heart holds a secret. We cheered. And Mother smiled.

A few moments later, we found another bullet, which had dug a hole through the headboard of the only bed in the room. It was buried inside the headboard's two metal layers. The slightest move made it rattle noisily. Every night before the war, my brothers and I had vied to sleep in that bed. We had settled on taking turns. Now we could not remember whose turn it had been on the day we left. From that night on, however, we pulled the mattress off the bed frame. No matter whose turn it was, we would sleep on the ground.

Searching the room for more bullets, we realized that we had no matches to light the kerosene lamp or the three-legged stove. Darkness quickly set in. How could we go to our neighbors again? So Mother asked us to sit quietly. Throughout the long night, I listened to the sound of her anxious steps on the tile as she moved back and forth between the door and the window.

When the sun rose the next day, my brothers and I set out to search for matchsticks in the yard, on the hillsides, and on the road. Mother raised her hands and asked Allah to guide our steps. We found handfuls of intact bullets and filled our pockets with empty cartridges. We flipped rocks and found scorpions underneath them, tails standing up braided with poison. We plowed the earth with our fingers and eyes and searched sites of old fires, but we found no matches.

Then we remembered that our father once said he could start a fire by rubbing two flint stones against each other. Flint stones were everywhere, round and smooth like balls of dough. Basel broke one into two pieces. Its inside was purple and glittered as though it were a tiny piece of starry sky. He struck its two sides, but no sparks appeared.

None of us wanted to go back to Mother without a match or some fire. We trusted that God was going to help because Mother had asked Him to do so, and we needed His help. So we remained outside until the sun finally went to sleep, tucking itself under the thin sheet of the horizon.

The possibility of finding a match now seemed as distant as the sky above us. We walked back silently, shuffling our feet and wondering if God was unhappy with us. But suddenly, our prayer seemed to have been answered with more than the sparks we had asked for. We heard footsteps in the distance. A shadowy figure was walking on the gravel road. It was Father.

He brought us food, a large bottle of water, pockets full of melon seeds as a treat—and matches. We competed to show him the bullets in the thermos and the bed. "Soldiers must have combed the city house by house," he said, shaking his head. After a long-awaited meal in the safety of our father's presence, and a few rides on his back around the room, we all lay on the mattresses like matchsticks, our laughter spreading like fire among us.

With borrowed money, Father bought us more food, including a giant can of Nido Nestlé powdered milk, which Mother struggled to keep away from our hungry hands. My brothers and I kept trying to reach into the can to eat the sweet powder, which tasted like candy.

In a short time, my parents cleaned the water-storage room. An elephant-size tanker then wobbled down the narrow gravel road and parked by our home. A man planted a giant pipe into the room and replenished the supply of water. Now we had enough to last us until December, when the rains would arrive.

Father found a job driving a truck for the Public Works Department. He said he was going to help repair roads destroyed by the war and to build new ones. Mother let us play outside as long as we remained within the reach of her voice. Once again, I could wait for my father at the end of the day. After dinner, I would wring my hands in delight and fear as he told us his favorite stories of buried treasures, taking us on endless thrilling journeys as he spoke. Our family seemed to be quickly returning to life as we'd known it. And now that Basel and Muhammad had decided I was old enough to play with them, I was happier than ever.

To celebrate their regained freedom, my brothers wanted to build a kite. The November wind would not stop them. Basel and Muhammad had learned how to make kites from the Mahasreh boys before they stopped talking to us. Now, my brothers asked our father for reed stalks for the kite's skeleton. Alarmed, he said the kite might get us in trouble with the Mahasreh if it got tangled in their trees. But my brothers begged and pleaded, promising we would cause no trouble, until finally Father brought some common reeds and cut them into thin spokes for us.

Basel and Muhammad then begged Mother for dough. They needed glue and knew that sticky dough would work as a substitute. She gave them the dough and also some torn-up pieces of cloth that would become the kite's tail.

They measured the spokes, making certain they were of identical lengths, then wrapped a thread that turned the spokes into an eight-angled star with a perfect center. Using the dough, they glued the star to brown paper, attached streamers that gave the kite its whiskers, and added the tail. They would launch it in the morning.

The next day Basel held the kite's ball of string, steering it right and left the way my father steered a truck. Muhammad carried the kite, ran with it, then let it glide on the wind. The kite zigzagged and quickly took to the sky. We all ran, screaming encouragements to make it rise higher. It did.

Finally my brothers let me hold the kite string for a moment. The soaring kite was heavier than I had expected. It was stronger than I was and pulled me forward. But I pulled the string back. It was a wonderful new feeling. I was thrilled to show my brothers that they had been right to trust me to share in their games. Holding that string, I felt as though I owned a piece of the sky.

I returned the string to Basel and continued to gaze upward. The kite held us in its spell, our heads back, mouths wide open, eyes dancing with every flicker, when suddenly we felt the earth shake under our feet and heard a strange sound. It was loud and thudding, as though someone were knocking from inside the earth. "*Hazzah ardeyyah!*" Basel said. "An earthquake!" We looked down at our feet but saw nothing. Then we glanced up the road. There was the source of the earth-shaking noise.

From the mouth of the gravel road emerged a long line of Israeli soldiers. They moved in pairs, shoulder to shoulder, stomping forcefully, chanting at the top of their lungs. And they carried guns.

Where were they going? There were no other homes on that road. Were they coming for us?

Basel let go of the kite; he gave it to the wind, and we bolted for home.

"Hide!" shouted Mother. We pushed our Formica cupboard up to the door and pressed against it with our bodies as the noise got closer and closer, until it was surrounding us, engulfing our home.

When we peeked out the window, the entire length of the road was a blur of khaki interrupted only by the white and blue of the Israeli flag. Now we could see the soldiers, and we knew that if any one of them turned his head, he could see us, too. But none did. They moved in the same direction, like one long dragon, hundreds of heads covered with half-watermelon khaki helmets strapped under hundreds of chins, and hundreds of stomping feet, all wearing high leather boots.

Reaching the hill, the soldiers spread out. We glued ourselves to our window to watch every move they made. They dug trenches, hid inside them, pulled up green thornbushes by the roots, put them on their helmets, raised their heads, shot in the air, hid again. A bullet came near our house; it whistled and whizzed as a stone repelled it. Land Rovers created clouds of dust while a helicopter hovered above the soldiers.

Had the fighting started again? I put on my shoes and laced them tightly. I had just turned four, and I needed no one to tell me what to do when I heard the sounds of war.

Jerusalem

For three weeks, we were unable to go outside our house. The soldiers came to the hill in the morning and left in the late afternoon. They set up cardboard people and fired at them for hours. The sounds of the bullets filled my mind. I could hear bullets being fired long after the soldiers were gone. I even heard bullets in my sleep.

Mother complained that spending all day and night with us in a tiny room was giving her gray hair even though she was only twenty-four. "Gray hair? Show us," we said. That made her even more furious. But it was our father, at forty-four, who really had gray hair, and a few white hairs, too.

Father said white hair meant that a person was wise. His own white hairs clearly allowed him to know many things, including what the Israeli soldiers were doing around our house. He called it *munawarat*, training for combat. The soldiers were also conquering the territory, studying the hill in order to fight well on it, he explained.

But that made no difference to Mother. She was becoming more and more impatient, even hitting us if we went near the windows. Terrified of stray bullets, she complained about the windows so much that I no longer knew whether it was a good or a bad thing for a house to have them.

She also tried to stop us from playing war. But we liked our pretend wars. We imitated the soldiers, pointing our fingers or pointing bananas, spoons, or slippers at one another and making the sounds of shooting. Acting injured, we swayed and landed on our backs. We pretended we were dead for a moment, got up, and started the sounds of make-believe shooting again.

Mother did not seem to be mad at the soldiers who were shooting real bullets. Instead, she was mad at us! She cried when we talked back to her and shouted that we wanted a place outside to play. She cried while she nursed Maha, changed our clothes, and cooked our meals. If I asked her why she was crying, she would impatiently say it was onion that made her cry, even if she had no onions near her.

She had told me over and over that crying led to blindness. Did Mother want to become blind and not see the world outside our window? She seemed so anxious and sad. Then in the beginning of December, she made up her mind that she no longer wanted to live in a house that had become a prison.

"I'll go anywhere as long as it is far away from here," she told Father. He became angry. They spoke for hours, until she finally said that she wanted to take us to the Dar El-Tifl orphanage in Jerusalem.

"Orphanage?" Father exclaimed. "Our children are not orphans!"

"But you cannot protect them," Mother shot back.

Father pounded the wall. "They are not orphans. They are not orphans," he kept saying as he watched us gather our belongings.

I did not want to leave. I wanted to see my father every day and hold his big hand every chance I got. There would be no treats, no back rides, no truck rides, and no after-dinner stories about treasures without him.

I did not want to say he was dead. So I decided that if someone asked about him I would say I didn't know where he was. "Ask Mother," I would say. Before we left, I built a stone person, a *qantara*, behind our house and told Dad that it was to remind him that I loved him each time he saw it.

At Dar El-Tifl, Mother looked the head administrator in the eye and said that Father had died in the war. The words made me ill. My father had become a secret.

We were admitted to the orphanage. In exchange, Mother would live on-site, care for infant orphans, and help staff a demanding night shift. During the day, she attended classes or studied. Mother's dream was to become more and more educated. It hardly mattered what she studied, as long as she was learning.

Winter came, and the cold at Dar El-Tifl dug deep into my flesh and lingered below my ragged clothes. It left me and all the other children trembling, coughing, and crying for warmth, our noses red. Now I felt as though I had lost both of my parents, for I hardly saw my mother.

Nights at Dar El-Tifl were scary and long. Shadows of blankets, beds, and clothes looked like monsters. And to move meant to attract their attention. I wet my bed every night rather than leave it and cross the dimly lit yellow hallways to the bathroom. Wetting the bed warmed me up for a few moments, then kept me shivering until the morning. Many other children wet their beds, too, and every morning the bedrooms smelled like a barn and the sheets piled up like mountains in the laundry room.

Daily, we ate three small meals. After we had brought our empty plates back to the kitchen window, we were still hungry. We exchanged glances and sighs. There were no second helpings, and there was nothing to eat in between. Each meal was served at a set time. If you missed it, you had to fill your growling belly with water until the next meal. I ate the food that was given to me, not because I liked it but because our teachers were monitoring our every move. The exception was the falafel balls and sesame bread, which were served for breakfast once a week and tasted like treats compared with anything else we were given. Most of all, I was thankful we didn't always have to eat lentils.

My brothers were placed with the six- and seven-year-old children, my sister with the one-year-olds and toddlers. I was put in preschool with the other four-year-olds. My classroom had a blackboard in it and lying in its tray was a piece of chalk. "Alef!" I cried out. I ran to the board, wanting to pick him up, hold him, take him with me. But my teacher came between us, saying that only she could use the chalk. I followed her hand, Alef swinging back and forth in it. When she was done, she put Alef on the table. He rolled off and broke into pieces.

In this class I did not speak with Alef, but I learned about two new members of his family, Ba and Ta. They lived with him. I wished I could live with Alef, Ba, and Ta, for I felt so alone and afraid at Dar El-Tifl.

Only the half hour of recess, when I could be with my brothers, made me feel safer. When the bell rang and the children hurried outside, my brothers and I met. I wanted to play with them, but they had games to play with those in their own classes.

I spent much of my time bending over and looking at my brothers and the playground upside down. I imitated those who squealed with excitement as they hung from two parallel bars I could not reach.

Things changed when a boy punched me in the face and made my nose bleed. He wanted to fight my brothers but knew they were strong and were always together. So he hit me instead. Seeing what happened, my brothers charged toward him. They caught him and dragged him to where I stood.

They kicked him, twisted his arms, slapped his face, and muffled his mouth. They asked me to tell them when to stop. They said they would hit him until I said *khalas*, enough. When I finally did, the boy sat up crying. His nose was bleeding now, too. Teachers took me and the boy off the playground. We lay down side by side, held our noses to stop the bleeding, and struggled to breathe.

The weekend following the fight, my brothers were expelled from Dar El-Tifl with no warning for having beaten up this boy and having had fights with other children. They were always ready for a fight on the playground, and Mother was too busy to keep track of all of us. So on an early February day, my brothers were sent to an all-boys orphanage in Jericho.

Horrified, I ran after the car that took them away. But the giant school gate clanged shut as the car left. I hit the gate over and over and shouted that I wanted to go with them.

Then I went to find Maha, who, having just learned how to walk, toddled like a duck. She was too young for me to talk to, but I felt better just sitting with her. Her teacher, though, said I must go to my own class. Now, it seemed only Alef remained in my world.

That night, while everyone slept, I stayed awake, stiff with fear and sadness. The night monsters appeared even bigger. But suddenly I left my bed and tiptoed through my fear until I reached the steps. I walked to my classroom.

Inside, a round moon met me, shining through the square window, its yellow light spreading like a rug under my feet. I stood in the lemony silence wondering, Will the moon tell on me? Then I walked to the blackboard and tapped on the chalk.

"I need you, Alef," I whispered. I told him what had happened and how sad I felt.

Alef and I arrived at a plan. If it succeeded, I would be reunited with my brothers. Disobeying my teacher's orders, I planted Alef deep in my pocket and returned to bed.

The next day at recess I watched everyone play. I imagined my brothers were with me. I stood aside for a long time, then ran to the classroom, where Alef and I carried out the first step of our plan. Before the bell rang and my classmates lined up to resume the school day, I tore up all the notebooks on their desks. Then I sat waiting.

My teacher was astonished. She asked me to stand, and with a wooden pointer she hit the backs of my hands till I thought my fingers were going to break. I did not move. I kept my hands open as I cried. She ordered that I stand in the corner and raise my hands against the wall. In defiance, I smiled to the wall the way my brothers had taught me to do after Father or Mother hit us. They told me this showed that on the inside they were never broken, no matter how bad the pain.

After my brothers were expelled, I found something in the school to tear up every day for a week. And every day I was hit. But one day a smiling woman came in, asked for me, and took me to the playground. She wondered out loud why I tore up things in the school. "Why act like unruly boys?" she asked.

I told her that I wanted to be expelled and sent to where my brothers were. "I want my brothers!" I exploded.

She understood. "If you tear up nothing for a month, I will arrange for you to visit your brothers in Jericho," she promised. So I returned to my quiet ways and to learning more of the alphabet. I learned other things, too, including that a month was thirty days. I counted each passing day. And I hoped that the woman would keep her promise.

Jericho

The month was over and the promise was kept. Mother dressed me and Maha and combed our hair. We were ready to go. I took along drawings I had made for this day. In all of them, Basel, Muhammad, and I stood holding hands.

Right outside Dar El-Tifl's gate I found a surprise—Father! The sleeves of his shirt were rolled up as though he was going to work. But he was here to take us to Jericho. Seeing his smile erased the final traces of my sadness. Looking at the street, cars, trees, and people from inside his arms, I knew I never wanted to go back to Dar El-Tifl.

At the taxicab station for Jericho, Father bought a box of marshmallow-chocolate mounds. He offered me one, but I wanted to save them all for my brothers. Settling in the seat of a taxi, I held the box in my lap, guarding it as I guarded my drawings.

"If you feel pressure on your eardrums, open your mouth," the taxi driver announced.

"Jericho is eight hundred feet below sea level," Father explained to us. "Half an hour and we will get there," he said.

When we arrived in Jericho it did feel like a different world. Though it was only the beginning of March, the weather was so hot the car felt like a teakettle with all of us boiling and sweating inside. Touching the car's metal door stung my skin.

The boys' orphanage, called Al-Bir Society, was at the edge of the Aqabat Jaber refugee camp. Mother mentioned that Aqabat Jaber was one of the largest Palestinian refugee camps. Many of Al-Bir's orphans came from this camp. She knew because the second year she and my father were married they had lived in Aqabat Jaber. Muhammad was born in this camp, but unlike many camp residents my parents were able to move out before I was born.

"One can die of heatstroke any day in this desert," Father said. When the taxi let us out in front of the gate, sand was everywhere.

This orphanage had walls bigger than those enclosing Dar El-Tifl. Al-Bir's walls were made to stop strangers from entering the orphanage as well as boys from running away. My father knocked at the big gate. I extended my arms out straight, holding the candy box topped with the drawings.

An older guard with a head cover opened the gate and

beckoned us in. We gave him my brothers' names. Father said he was their uncle.

The guard seemed pleased to see us. He said he was happy each time any of the boys had a visitor. He went to call my brothers, who were asleep. We had arrived during their compulsory afternoon nap time.

I anxiously waited near the guard's chair, watching every step he took as he crossed the huge, empty playground and entered a door at the center of the building. Everything seemed asleep, wilted by the heat.

I looked at the dozens of windows and doors, and wondered if Basel and Muhammad were really inside. Everything was so quiet. Then, suddenly, they appeared. They woke up the world with their shouts of surprise and excitement. And as they approached us, I ran toward them across the thirty days of waiting and wondering if I would ever see them again, across the thirty days of feeling alone without them.

Basel and Muhammad's heads were shaved. They had become very thin. Without waiting for questions, they began to talk about everything. They tugged at our clothes, pulled our hands, wanted us to listen with more than our ears. I gave them the marshmallow mounds, which had melted in the Jericho heat. They ate everything at once, for anything that remained would be stolen by the other boys.

Now it was time to give them my drawings, and they gazed at them with the same hunger they'd had when they ate. "This is me!" said Muhammad, pointing to a stick fig-

ure with greenish eyes. I stood proud when everyone confirmed that the three stick figures holding hands in my
drawings looked like the three of us.

My brothers, too, had brought gifts. They asked that I
close my eyes and open my hands. In one hand Muhammad
put a ring he said he had found on the playground the first
day he and Basel were brought to Al-Bir. He'd hid it in his
pocket all this time so no one would steal it. In my other
hand Basel put a *ta'reefeh*, a penny, which he had gotten
from somewhere.

"We knew you'd be coming to see us," Basel said.
"We've waited for you every day."

Happiness filled my heart. I put the ring on my finger
and the *ta'reefeh* in my pocket. I stood in the middle, my
brothers holding my hands. It was as though we were standing in one of my drawings.

The principal said we could not take my brothers outside
the school grounds. He pointed to a wooden bench at the
edge of the playground and said we could sit there if we
wanted to, or we could go inside. But he warned us to be
quick, because some boys who never had visitors became sad,
jealous, or hostile when they saw other boys with company.

Basel and Muhammad wanted us to go inside and see
the world they lived in before we all sat outside to visit.
They led us into the cafeteria, then into their sleeping area,
with bunk beds in long rows. They pointed to sleeping boys
and whispered. One boy named Roubine tried to run away
from the orphanage daily. On the days he succeeded in getting outside the gate, he waited for a bus to stop, then hung

on its back rails. He changed buses, continually hanging on the back, until he reached Jerusalem. Bus drivers captured and returned him.

Basel and Muhammad had adjacent beds, but shaking their heads in horror for lack of words, they began to tell us what went on at Al-Bir. Every night, they said, some hostile boys rolled sand in paper to create what they called sand cigarettes and waited until everyone slept, then went around putting the sand cigarettes in the mouths of snoring boys. The snorers would choke and almost die. So every night, afraid to sleep alone, my brothers crawled into one bed and slept back to back. On nights when the desert temperature dropped sharply, it became impossible for them to fall asleep because of the cold. So they stayed awake and cried.

When we went outside and sat in the shade of a tree, my brothers confessed they frequently got hit, often unfairly, they assured us. They begged that we take them back with us. My parents grew silent. They seemed shattered by what they had heard, but what could they do?

Then my father spoke. "Mirriam! Let's take them out."

"Take them out to where?" she replied.

"Our children are treated like orphans while we live," he said, lowering his voice in order not to attract attention.

"You want us to go back to that prison on the hill?" she hissed, now weeping. "You try it—stay with four children in a tiny room all day while soldiers are shooting outside. You try it," she pressed.

My father shook his head and cursed the world. Then he thought for a moment. "What if I build a wall in front of the house?" he begged. "I can ask a few of my friends to help me. We can do it in no time. And it would cover the big window. The soldiers would not be able to see us from the road."

But Mother was still not convinced.

"I can also keep the water supply replenished and connect it to a hose to reach the kitchen so you won't need to go outside for water," he argued.

Mother still resisted.

"What if I purchase a goat for milk and chickens for eggs, and build a shed for the animals? That will make life easier for you," he begged.

"But what if I still don't feel safe in that wretched house?" she challenged.

"I would not ask you to live there for a moment longer," he said.

Mother finally softened. "Let us go back just for a while and see," she bargained. "But only when the summer vacation begins."

We left Basel and Muhammad at Al-Bir orphanage, their faces pale with disappointment. The guard reminded them to wipe away their tears so they would not look like girls. The end of the school year felt far away, like a country at the end of the world. But if I was patient and waited, I would reach it and see my brothers again. I had waited before. I would wait again.

On the first day of June, Father stood at Dar El-Tifl's gate holding hands with my brothers. He had picked them up earlier. We all rode back home together, Father singing loudly as he drove. "Wait until you see your house," he kept telling us. His voice was full of smiles. But Mother was quiet.

When we arrived we found a house different from the one we had left. A brick wall concealed the front window. It connected to the sides of the house and made an extra outside room. Grapevines spread on wire to create a roof and block the summer sun. Water now reached the kitchen through a hose with a nozzle that opened and closed with a simple twist. It also reached the plot of vegetables Father had planted in preparation for our arrival: carrots, tomatoes, parsley, zucchini, onions, eggplants, and melons. He had watered them daily. All had thrived. The watermelons were the size of gum balls. In a few weeks they would be larger than soccer balls.

Two geranium pots stood by the entrance. Mother crushed the leaves between her fingers, breathed in the fragrance, and smiled. I stuck the round red petals on my toenails so they looked like Mother's painted nails during the Eid holiday celebration.

Father had also built a shed on the left side of the house. The promised goat was inside it; we heard her bleating. We raced to the shed to look at her. She was large and had banana-shaped horns. Her eyes were the shape of peanuts, and her hair was brown with apricot-blond streaks. She was a *Shameyyah* goat, he boasted. That meant she was imported from Syria. "She can bear baby goats twice a year if fed well," he said. The goat's belly already held a baby that would soon be born.

Father put his arm around Mother's shoulders, and

we all walked to the backyard overlooking the valley. He pointed to the stone person I had built for him before I left for Dar El-Tifl. I jumped into his arms and let him carry me.

We sat on the red earth, talking and laughing, the setting sun a bonfire before us. My father picked up tiny pebbles and flung them into the distance, just like he always used to do.

My heart knew that this was my true home. Unlike the many places we had lived in since the war changed our lives, this was the place I loved. I knew the road to it, and knew where the road led to beyond it. The skin of my bare feet recognized the skin of the red earth with all its wrinkles. The thornbushes often pricked me, but I knew how to pull out the thorns. And I liked to walk around the miniature pyramid-like mounds of fresh earth dug out by the moles. I knew the weak-sighted moles were there even if I had never seen them.

Night in this place filled me with fear, but that fear ended in the morning and I got used to the rhythm of fear coming to my heart and leaving it. I began to identify the sounds of night crickets as star sounds because the stars and the crickets came out together. One twinkled to the ear, the other to the eye.

And I knew the breeze that trekked from the bottom of the hill and flew into our windows. It filled the curtains with a daily dance and softly kissed my face. Flapping my arms to let the breeze tickle me, for a moment I felt free, like a bird, tasting the sky. All here was mine, and felt like home to me. Sitting silently, I knew for sure that I did not want to leave this place ever again, no matter what Mother decided.

Accident

The soldiers continued to come to the hill, but now they trained farther away from our home. We could see their helmets appear and disappear in the distance. At night, a giant beam of light like an endless sword scraped from one end of the sky to the other. It looked like the longest windshield wiper ever, and it whipped our house and windows. It lit our faces for seconds as it slashed through. "This is a searchlight," my father said. "It helps soldiers monitor the area at night."

"What if they see something they don't like?" I asked.

"They will attack," he replied.

Because there was no electricity in our home or around us, the searchlight was astounding. Thinking about faraway soldiers watching us, I wondered whether I was sleeping right, and whether those soldiers could see inside my mind that I was upset with what they were doing. I did not want them to come to our house, especially at night. So I stopped myself from thinking about the light, covered my head, and tried to fall asleep. But the light was powerful—it lit up the entire room whenever it suddenly appeared. It woke me up again and again until my brothers and I invented games about it—guessing when it would come and how many times a night it would return. When we were done playing, we slept on our faces and pulled pillows over our heads.

Not wanting to be alone either day or night, Mother came up with a plan to fill our house with company while Father was gone during the day. She had sewn since she was a young girl and had taken additional classes at Dar El-Tifl. Now she told our relatives, her friends, and distant neighbors in the Irsaal area at the bottom of the hill that she would tailor clothes for them. Soon, our home was full of women and children who nicknamed Mother "Mirriam Al-Jabaleyyah," Mirriam of the Mountain, because they had to climb the big hill to reach our house. Every day our floor was carpeted with colorful rolls of fabric, yarn, sewing patterns, and issues of *Burda*, a fashion magazine.

Burda was written in German, a language taught at Dar El-Tifl. Mother could not read or speak German, but she used the sewing patterns as though she understood every word. I gazed at the *Burda* pages, with their pictures of girls who stood next to their bicycles, carried flowers in baskets, smiled, and wore new dresses and shoes. They had long, golden braids that rested on their backs.

"How beautiful!" Mother exclaimed. "Green and blue eyes, and skin white like milk."

None of the *Burda* girls looked like me. My hair and eyes were the color of coffee. But I wanted to be exactly like them, so that I might have new dresses, shoes, and especially a bicycle.

Our Singer sewing machine worked by pushing a pedal. Mother sat in a chair and pumped the pedal up and down with her feet while her hands steered the stitches on wedding and maternity dresses, children's clothes, pajamas, and skirts. People laughed happily as they twirled around in front of the narrow mirror and saw themselves in their new clothes. Everyone said that Mother's sewing was better than anything purchased from a store.

Mother's sewing business grew. More and more fabrics were spread out on the floor of our home until she needed the entire space for her sewing. We moved our play outside—under the grapevines within the wall Father had built.

If we hit one another while we were playing and distracted her, Mother warned that she would give us to the Yahood, the Jews. The only Jews we knew were the Israeli soldiers. "Take this one; I want to get rid of him," she would say, pretending to give us away.

Soon Mother seemed to give up and let us play in the front yard more often, then outside our wall, on the road. Gradually, we felt that she was not afraid for us anymore. Her only rules were that we must wait to go outside the wall until the light fell against our house with an angle that signified four o'clock. Mother, who did not have a watch, judged time by the sun and the lengths of shadows. Before four, she said, venomous snakes and scorpions roamed in the heat. The second rule was that the three of us must be together at all times. I was happy with that rule.

Basel and Muhammad made paper rockets and kites. We searched under rocks, amid thorns, and under trees for any abandoned materials we could turn into parts for toys we would invent. Everything could be used—cans, metal pieces, broken glass, wild animal bones, or bells that fell from the necks of goats herded by shepherds. And with each passing day, we dared to go closer to the soldiers, until one afternoon we stood only yards away and could look into their faces.

They motioned for us to leave. We retreated for a few minutes, then returned. We had become more curious than scared. What intrigued me most was how soldiers, clutching wide-open umbrellas, jumped from flying planes and landed on the ground unharmed.

When the soldiers left every evening, we searched the countless trenches they had dug, climbed the barbed-wire fences they had erected, dragged home the cardboard people that were left standing pierced everywhere with bullet holes, filled our pockets with empty bullet cartridges, and glared at the huge amounts of food the soldiers threw away. But Mother warned us not to eat any of the chocolate spreads, jams, sliced breads, or cookies, or drink any of the chocolate milk in the cartons the soldiers regularly left behind. "It could poison you," she said. And so we never ate or drank any of it.

One afternoon, as we were searching the grounds, my brothers found a gun. "A Sten!" they shouted. The soldiers had left it behind. It was so heavy it took both of them to lift it up. Basel held the front end, the metal barrel, and Muhammad held the back. We began to walk home carrying it as though it were a deer we had hunted. But only moments later, a jeep filled with soldiers arrived. They shouted and gestured to my brothers to drop the gun. Then they took it and left.

Gradually, when we returned from our adventures, Mother stopped asking us where we had been. She knew. She mended our clothes torn by the barbed-wire fences, daubed our cuts and scrapes with iodine, and shook her head.

Like my brothers and me, the soldiers were always in groups. They came and left together. But one day a soldier appeared in a jeep after everyone else had left. We were surprised to see him. He was speeding and appeared not to know that the gravel road swerved, then dead-ended shortly past our house. We watched. When the jeep reached the end and took a sharp turn, it spun around and landed on its side.

"Accident!" we all exclaimed. We instantly wanted to know what had happened to the driver, so we raced to the site. But when we were only a few yards away, we stopped.

We looked into one another's eyes for courage to move closer. What if he was dead? We held on to one another's clothes and inched forward till we could see him. His chest was caught under the steering wheel.

We knocked at the jeep's window. He looked up, able to move only a hand. Dressed in his khaki uniform and helmet, he looked like a helpless turtle flipped upside down. He whimpered, then spoke faintly. We did not understand him and replied in anxious, loud voices, asking him what he needed. He did not understand us either.

But when he pointed his thumb to his open mouth, we knew what he wanted. We ran home and hurried back with a bucket of drinking water. But how could we reach him to help him drink?

Before we could decide what to do, another jeep tore down the gravel road, and then other vehicles followed. "*Rooh lebaitak*," someone said to us, ordering us to go home. But we did not want to go. Instead we watched from a distance as the injured soldier was pulled out of the jeep, placed on a stretcher, and taken away.

The wrecked jeep remained abandoned for two days. We wanted to play inside it but were afraid, so we only circled it. Finally, a truck with a winch hauled it away like a dead animal. It left a hole in the ground that kept the image of the jeep alive in our minds every time we passed it. We described the accident to one another over and over. And we hoped that the wounded soldier would live and heal.

I realized then that the Israeli soldiers had become part of our daily life. We watched them, imitated them, puzzled over their actions, and talked about them all the time. They were the source of our anxiety and our entertainment.

The day of that accident was also the day I began to worry about my father. He drove a truck for long hours. Sometimes he fell asleep at the wheel and told us about it when he came home. Sometimes he even took one of my brothers with him, to wake him up if he nodded off.

I could see him in my mind, driving in the summer heat, his sleeves rolled up, his elbow always showing from the window. I worried he might fall asleep one day, lose control of his truck, have a wreck, be injured. He would be alone, wanting water, unable to drink it. And who would help him?

Zuraiq

Our ten black chickens and the red-brown rooster arrived in a cage. A man with a golden tooth that glittered when he spoke released them into the garden. They jumped out, flapping their wings, and immediately pecked the ground for anything to eat. At night, they shared the shed with the goat.

From the day of his arrival, the rooster changed the rhythm of our mornings. He was up at dawn and woke everyone with him. My father liked the rooster's call because it helped him perform his morning prayers on time. Father prayed five times a day. He would spread a tiny rug that had a drawing of a mosque on it, stand up facing in the direction of Mecca, and then bow to God, kneeling and leaning forward until his forehead touched the ground. That was the moment my brothers, sister, and I liked to jump on his back. Then he would laugh and raise his voice but never stop praying. We knew he wouldn't because he had told us that during prayer one steps inside the hand of God. I felt like we were climbing inside the hand of God with him.

The rooster continued his calls long after Father's prayers were over. I did not like how persistent he was in wanting no one to sleep past the time he was up. But I liked how the feathers on his tail stood up straight, and how his posture was proud, almost like that of a soldier—our own soldier. He walked like a king with his tomato-red crown. As he strutted, I wanted to strut just like him.

I found Mother's lipstick and colored my face red. I put on her only pair of high heels and walked about holding my head high, raising each foot the way the rooster did. I would suspend my foot in the air, pause, then lower and rest it fully on the ground. I snapped my head back as though I had accomplished a great task, then glanced left and right at the chickens to make sure they saw me.

Unlike the rooster, the chickens were mostly quiet, except when they cackled to announce that an egg would soon be laid. My brothers, sister, and I answered the cackles. We collected most of the eggs while they were still warm. But we always left a few to hatch.

The hand-size baby chickens were most exhilarating to Maha. She jumped up and down when she saw one peck its way out of a shell. And the chicks were beautiful—even more beautiful than the eggs when we boiled them in onion peels and herbs to color them. We held the baby chickens with utmost care, for they were fragile—like candles in the wind. I did not want any of the chicks to die. But many did die, from the summer heat or from snakebites; some even died the very day they hatched. I buried them beside the shed, covering their bodies with leaves.

On some Fridays, however, Mother and Father killed an adult chicken for a feast to celebrate our being together, and having survived one more week of our tumultuous life. Friday, *Jumua*, meaning the day of gathering, was our weekly day off. We ate meat only on Fridays. My dad often bought us a fresh piece of lamb or goat meat from the butcher shop. But the chickens that we ate came from the ones we raised.

After choosing the chicken to be killed, Father tied its wings to its back and handed the head to Mother. She pulled it, exposing the neck as he said a short prayer, then ran a knife through it. Mother always grimaced, pursed her lips, and shut her eyes as the knife moved. I covered my face with my hands. Father then threw the chicken aside, and its blood splattered everywhere. The chicken's headless body ran in blind circles until the blood surge slowed and the body pulled up dead—right before us.

Mother boiled the chicken to loosen the feathers before she plucked them and opened up the cavity. She pulled out the heart, the liver, and what looked like a stomach pouch, and cleaned and fried them as a side dish. She spent half the day cooking before the meal was finally served. The remainder of the day was for resting from a week of work.

My jobs were to help with Maha and keep an eye on the

chickens so they wouldn't stray or get snatched by foxes or wild dogs. Maha would call the chicks to come to her. When they didn't, she would run after them, but by the time she had balanced herself, they got away. She ran and squatted again and again, calling them with strange made-up names. Trying to teach her the right words only made her come up with words that sounded more and more peculiar.

I also watched the goat, which had now grown so large she almost touched both sides of the door when she entered or left the shed. The goat silently ate whatever we gave her, and in the afternoon she sat still, continuing to chew as if she had imaginary food in her mouth.

My brothers and I decided to pick out a name for the baby in the goat's belly before it was born. We wanted a name that would make our father happy. But nothing came to mind. So we asked him to help us. Father had no trouble picking out the name. He simply pointed to the faraway horizon and said "Zuraiq," meaning "Little Blue." We understood.

Father often pointed to the horizon behind our home. He said if we squinted hard enough, especially on sunny days, we could glimpse the Mediterranean Sea. It would look like a little blue line scribbled along the horizon. He spoke as though that "little blue line" were a thread of magic. He said he had lived and worked in the city of Jaffa by the Mediterranean for many years before the war of 1948, and the sight of any of us squinting hard to see Jaffa's sea filled him with happiness, as though it was him in Jaffa we longed to see.

I told the goat that we were going to name her baby Zuraiq. Her response was nothing more than twitching her ear and continuing to chew her imaginary food. She never responded much to me or to my brothers, but whenever she saw our father, she tried to run to him just as we did, held back only by the rope and peg that leashed her.

She stopped tugging at her rope when he entered the house. She knew he soon would be making certain her food and water pots were filled. After dinner he would spend a long time combing her hair and humming his favorite songs to her. He would confide in her, telling her everything about his day.

But one day the goat cried in a strange way. She was inside the shed, staggering from wall to wall, her legs too thin for her full belly. Then, within moments of Father's arrival, her body opened up for the baby goat to come out. She bled, and lowered herself to the ground. Pointing her face to the ceiling, she bleated in pain. The head of the baby goat appeared. My father eased it out. The long neck, sock ears, chest, and folded front legs followed. Then came the back legs and the tiny tail. The mother goat turned around and licked her baby clean.

Father lifted up the baby goat's leg and announced that it was a boy. Basel, Muhammad, and I were speechless until the baby goat made its first tiny bleat. We bleated in return. Each of us reached out to touch him—thinking he would belong to the one who touched him first—and we all touched him at once. We named him Zuraiq, as we had planned.

Leaving Zuraiq and his mother to rest, we watched as Father buried the afterbirth in the backyard. When we returned, Zuraiq was struggling to stand. He was unable to balance himself on all four legs, so we held him up. He stood for a moment, then fell down. We held him up again and again until he took a step. When he finally walked a few steps all by himself, we cheered and clapped.

Nursing and playing were Zuraiq's main activities. Our father milked the mother goat only once in the first week, to let us taste the special richness of birth milk. After that, he milked her only in the evening, letting Zuraiq have his fill. But when Zuraiq could finally eat grass and grains, Father covered the mother goat's udders in order to wean Zuraiq.

On the day Zuraiq was weaned, we begged Father to promise he would not sell him or kill him on a Friday like a chicken, or for sacrifice meat on the Eid holiday. In a short time, Zuraiq had become a member of our family. Just as Father needed to talk to Zuraiq's mother, my brothers and I argued that we needed to talk to Zuraiq. Just as the mother goat bleated only when Father came home, Zuraiq ran only toward Basel, Muhammad, and me. He did everything we asked him to do, and he wanted to go with us anywhere we went. Father promised he would keep Zuraiq as a pet for us.

Each of us wanted to be with Zuraiq, but Basel and Muhammad would soon start their school year. Only when I had turned six would I be able to attend school. The thought that my brothers and I were going to be separated

one more time made me anxious, but I was happy that Zuraiq would become mine alone when my brothers were in
school.

So, amid protestations from my brothers, I called our
pet goat Zuraiqee, meaning "My Zuraiq." He began mostly
to follow me. And when he lay down in the shade to rest, he
even let me put my head on him and go to sleep as though
he were a pillow.

The night before September 1, when my brothers began school, Mother bathed us all in a wide tin tub the way
she did once every week. She set out my brothers' newly tai-
lored clothes for the first school day. She also ironed their
clothes, which she rarely did except on the sacred holidays.
But school and learning were just as sacred to Mother. As
she sprinkled water on the cloth and tilted her head right
and left to avoid the scalding steam, she and Father talked
to us about their own schooling.

"When I was a child, Palestine was under the rule of the
British," my father said. "I finished only first grade because
my family could not afford the sixteen-piastre school fee the
government then required. Sixteen piastres was a big sum of
money during the thirties. It took some families a whole
month to earn that amount. But I was eager for learning. I
studied an extra half year at a mosque when a man volun-
teered to teach boys elementary math, and I memorized
part of the Qur'an there—the chapter called 'Surat Ya
Seen.' I can still recite it by heart."

Proudly, Father went on to recite the entire five-page

chapter. We cheered when he finished. But he interrupted and said that we should never cheer after hearing sacred text recited. "Silence is the best expression of respect," he instructed. So we sat quietly until Mother spoke.

"I finished the sixth grade, but then my family could no longer afford to send me to school," she said. "Leaving school was one of the worst days of my life. I begged the principal to let me sit on the floor, hoping that would reduce the fee. I even offered to clean the school in exchange for being a student. But the principal refused. And so instead of going to school, I worked in Jerusalem to help support my family until, when I was fifteen, your father and I married." When she was done speaking, Mother had tears in her eyes.

"But, Mother, can you afford the school fees for us?" Muhammad asked.

"United Nations schools don't require fees for children of refugees," she replied, to my brother's great relief.

The next morning, Mother woke up with the rooster, made tea, fried several eggs for breakfast, and boiled others for my brothers to take to school. She baked bread on hot little stones we called *rathef* in the iron oven set over the three-legged stove. She also made *zaatar manaqeesh*, olive oil and oregano pizza.

I felt unhappy watching Basel and Muhammad get ready to leave. Mother and Father said school was so important. Why must I wait while my brothers went? I distracted myself by spinning boiled eggs on the tile floor—for I had learned from Mother that a boiled egg spins quickly while a raw one is slow.

Father was getting ready to accompany Basel and Muhammad to the elementary school at the Jalazone Camp for refugees. He would register them and show them the bus to take between home and school.

"Don't let the camp boys hit you," he kept telling them over and over. "Stay together," he instructed.

"Can I go, too, Yaba?" I pleaded. But my father let me walk only a little way before he asked that I stop. "Just a few more steps," I begged.

He agreed, explaining to me that my brothers would come home in a few hours. "The time will pass in the blink of an eye," he said. "It's not like Al-Bir orphanage," he assured me. "You can play with Maha, and you'll have Zuraiq all to yourself when they're gone," he reminded me. "But don't wander anywhere close to the soldiers," he warned. The next year, when I turned six, he promised, I could go with my brothers every day.

I nodded, holding back a storm of sorrow. I wanted to grow up quickly—to turn six, to go to school and learn, to be with my brothers. Now, my footsteps heavy with sadness, I walked back home with Zuraiqee. He brushed his head against me. I felt he was the only one who understood my heart. I stroked his long ears with all my affection and then exploded in tears.

Jalazone Boys' School

The school year progressed, and to my surprise, instead of separating me from Basel and Muhammad, it brought us closer together because they included me in their studies. When I asked a question, they competed to answer. And they showed me all the lessons and drawings in their books. The lines on the pages were planted with words that opened up like rows of flowers, each with a different shape. The many dots on the letters scattered like poppy seeds. I memorized everything my brothers taught me.

While Basel and Muhammad were in school, I played teacher with Zuraiqee as my pupil. I explained my lessons over and over. I bribed him by feeding him. I tried to make him pay attention by putting the paper right under his nose. Then he would try to eat it. Zuraiqee was a lazy student, I thought. But with or without Zuraiqee, I studied. That made the time pass quickly until my brothers came home.

My brothers brought with them pocketfuls of knowledge about words from their teachers, and they also learned from the Jalazone schoolboys how to make all kinds of wonderful toys—skateboards constructed from wooden boxes and junkyard wheels, miniature wire cars with broom-long steering columns. They picked up new games, too—cards, tic-tac-toe—and learned the best way to spin a top. The pink-and-white, red-and-green tops in their hands spun on the tile like whirling dancers.

But because Jalazone boys also fought often, some days my brothers came home trying to conceal puffed-up eyes, torn clothes, or long scratches across their faces. I listened to details of their fights—the punching, the kicking, and the cursing—the way my father listened to radio broadcasts of boxing matches of the American heavyweight champion, Muhammad Ali, his biggest hero. I tapped my feet in cheers when my brothers told me they had won, especially in fights with the two Kanash boys.

The Jalazone teachers used harsh discipline to keep their classes under control. They kicked the students, called them names, slapped them in the face, dragged them by the ears, whipped them, and struck their hands with wooden sticks and rulers. "*Yabayee!*" my brothers exclaimed. "How painful!"

The world of Jalazone boys felt cruel to me, but I still wanted to know every detail of my brothers' experiences. I memorized the names of the unkind teachers, the names of the lenient ones, the descriptions of boys who cried when hit and those whose faces "looked like monkeys eating sour grapes" as they fought to keep back their tears. The boys avenged their pain by ridiculing their teachers. Basel and Muhammad took great delight in describing the science teacher's nose; it was longer than the pointer he carried, they said. "He could smell trouble from the farthest corner in the room."

I learned more about the cruelty of Jalazone life from the infectious diseases my brothers brought home. Bloody patches appeared on their scalps and made their hair disappear. They cried in pain, wanting so much to scratch their heads.

Father washed the spots with herbal solutions, but they made no difference. Mother, who had learned to give injections from a doctor in Jerusalem, took out the syringe and the needle she owned and boiled them for a long time to purify them. She broke open one of the tiny penicillin bottles she often bought when she shopped at a pharmacy, and tried giving my brothers a penicillin injection. But this also failed, and the patches continued to spread. My parents talked about the money needed for a doctor's visit. They could not afford one for a month.

Then Father had an idea—to wash the sores with Dead Sea water. He had heard that this small sea had earned its name because no plants, fish, or animals could live in it. Maybe germs couldn't live in it either. He took my brothers to bathe there. They brought back a bottle of sea water, and morning and evening, my father cleaned the sores and daubed them with the salty solution. The tears in my brothers' eyes seemed more bitter than the water stinging their skin. But they stood still, hoping Father's guess would prove right. And it did. The patches dried up and disappeared. In no time, the hair returned. After that, my father brought home a barrel of Dead Sea water, thinking it would cure everything.

But water from the Dead Sea did not eliminate the tapeworms that filled my brothers' intestines and mine. We did not understand how dozens of foot-long white worms got into our bellies and made them ache. Finally, Father drove us all to a clinic in a tiny town named Al-Qubeibeh near Jerusalem.

We stood by a high window in the waiting area. Without a word, a somber woman slid the glass aside and handed each of us a large cup of castor oil. "Pinch your nose and drink it in one gulp—without taking a breath," she instructed. If we could not keep the oil down, we were to drink again.

The thick, yellowish liquid looked and smelled nauseating. But the ache in our bellies was worse. So Basel and Muhammad and I took deep breaths, tilted the cups to our lips, and blinked that we were ready. "On the count of three," Mother coached. When we heard the word *three*, we took big gulps. "Keep it down," Mother begged. We each received a piece of licorice candy and a faint smile from the woman because we were successful.

I worried about my brothers catching diseases that we

would find no cure for, especially since Mother was always talking about the deadliness of cholera, typhoid, tuberculosis, and other infectious diseases. And Basel talked about one of his classmates who had suddenly gotten ill and, within a week, died.

Jalazone Boys' School stories filled my mind. Now I could imagine all the details of my brothers' days. When the radio announced 10:00 a.m., I wondered if they had gotten into fights during recess and whether anyone had hit them. In the afternoon, I thought of them walking out of their school gate, passing by a soldier's jeep that they said sometimes waited at the edge of the Nablus road by their school.

When winter arrived, I pulled Mother's dress in worry each time lightning belted the ballooning clouds, spilling rain on the fields. The thunder sounded like bombs. When my brothers finally arrived home on stormy days, they were shivering, their teeth chattering like hail on glass, their clothes dripping puddles under them, their high plastic boots filled with water because we could not afford umbrellas.

On Fridays, when my brothers were home all day with me, the three of us would wait until the rain stopped and the sun broke through the clouds. Then we begged Mother to let us go outside. If the temperature was freezing, she did not let us leave the house unless we promised that we would stay nearby.

But one time, we snuck away. We had a secret goal—to see if the soldiers were still training on these frozen days. None were. But the deep trenches they had dug were filled with water, and ice had formed lids on top of them. The entire place was ours.

We rubbed our hands and cheeks, shook our bodies to make ourselves warm. The world was washed clean by the winter rain, and it felt new under and above us. We could see our breath dance out of our chests as we made up songs about the soldiers, who were afraid of winter.

I was twirling in exhilarated laughter when I suddenly fell into a trench. Before I could make a sound, the sheet of ice began to close over me. My feet could not feel the bottom of the trench, and my hands could not hold on to anything to pull myself up. Horrified, my brothers lay on the ground and frantically broke the ice with their fists. Shouting my name, they kept thrashing until they finally pulled me out.

As we were walking home, my clothes froze on my body. I shook so hard I could no longer walk or cry. Muhammad took off his socks and put them on my feet; then he and Basel took turns carrying me on their backs.

At home, I could not stop shaking. "Where did you go?" Mother grilled us.

"She fell in a puddle," my brothers said over and over.

I nodded in agreement.

Mother poured water into a bowl engraved with Qur'an prayers on the inside. She called it the bowl of trembling, *taset al-rajfeh*. If one drank from it, she believed, one got healed from heart-stopping fear.

She let the water sit in *taset al-rajfeh* for an hour to give the sacred words time to mix in thoroughly. Then, "Drink," she said, handing me the *taset*. But I could not drink. I had developed a fever and my throat had become sore. So she gave me an injection and kept me cool with a wet cloth she put on my forehead. She took my temperature repeatedly and cursed the world when my fever remained high.

Father helped by cupping my back because he believed it would purify my body. He dropped burning pieces of paper inside glass cups and turned them upside down against my skin. The fire instantly died, and only smoke remained. Somehow, the cups clung to my skin. He packed many cups on my back, and I had to keep still in order for them to stay in place. I hated those cups, but I let him do it. He let me sleep near him, covered me with his winter coat, and kept checking on me all night.

I recovered. But my brothers and I were not allowed to play outside again until winter turned into spring.

Trapped inside, I took my sister for rides around the room, told her made-up stories about a family of ants, and ran my fingertips over her open palm to tickle it as if my fingers were ant feet. I did not stop until, squeaking with laughter, she threw herself on the floor. I loved making Maha laugh. When it was time for her to eat and she made loud noises, banging her cup on the table, I joined her.

If she had no tailoring jobs, Mother knitted clothes for us, turned Father's old shirts and pants into new shirts and pants for my brothers, and sewed cloth bags for herb and dried fruit and vegetable storage. As she worked, Mother also listened to songs and programs on the zucchini-green battery-run radio my father bought after our old stove-size radio died and could not be fixed.

Rasa'el Shawq (Letters of Longing) was the program Mother listened to most faithfully. It aired the voices of Palestinian refugees who could not return home after the war of 1948 or the Six-Day War. They revealed the shreds of their lives and hoped that relatives, or anyone who knew them, would hear the news and pass it on. I hoped to hear Hamameh's voice sending a greeting to Mother. I knew that would make her very happy.

On this program, people mentioned the names of their newborns, children who had finished high school, couples who had married, and relatives who had died recently. Sometimes they broke into tears as they asked questions and begged for replies and for *tasareeh*, visiting permits. Though I recognized none of the voices, I broke into tears along with them, especially when I saw Mother crying quietly. Radio letters were the only way the refugees outside could reach their relatives in our occupied cities. Many ended their messages by saying *Tammenoona ankum*, "Please send us word to ease our worries."

Then Fairuz, the beloved Lebanese singer, wailed the show's theme song. "*Wa salami lakom*," she began,

> *Greetings, greetings:*
> *People in the occupied land—*
> *People who are planted*
> *In your homes like trees—*
> *My heart is with you,*
> *I send you regards of peace.*

Her voice was like a comforting hand, reaching from afar, easing the winter. She was singing about us.

Spring came with the songs of the new birds that arrived and the wild poppies that swayed in the wind. Mother opened the door, and I threw myself into the warmth, held the red flowers between my hands, and brushed my cheeks with their petals. Inside their cups the black spots were like tiny bits of tea someone had left from winter. I picked some for Maha.

Green buds on the tree branches were rolled up like bullets, and I ran my fingers over them. Daffodils, calla lilies, and tulips appeared like guests for a short time and left. But cyclamens were mine. They shot from under the rocks, unfurled their ears, and listened.

Spring also brought back the soldiers. Some seemed to be new to the hill. Occasionally, one or two of them wandered toward our home during the day and knocked at the door. The minute Mother heard the soldiers knock, she ran to the door to make sure it was securely locked. Father and Mother had agreed on a special knock so Mother could know for certain that it was him. If the soldiers came to the window, she pointed to the water room outside, just in case they were looking for water. If they continued to speak, she furrowed her brow, raised her shoulders, and gestured that she did not understand them even if she did. They soon left.

The school year finally ended, and Basel and Muhammad raced home carrying their certificates. They both had passed. Mother was thrilled, and her arms fluttered like wings, reaching out to embrace them.

We had a picnic in the backyard, and Basel and Muhammad showed us their certificates and grades. An Alef meant "excellent." My father brought home *kullaj* and *kunafah* pastries to celebrate my brothers' success. Now only summer separated me from going to school every morning with them. But summer came with its own strange surprises.

Balad

"The time we've been looking forward to has come," Father told Mother one evening as he drank his sweet spearmint tea. "Now that Basel has turned eight and Muhammad seven, our boys are old enough to be circumcised," he said. Mother answered with a smile.

"We'll have a big celebration for them," he announced.

"What is circumcision?" I asked. I had heard the word before but had never really understood it. My question floated into my parents' sudden silence and hung like a bubble in the air. Mother dismissed it by saying that only boys are circumcised.

"What happens to a boy when he gets circumcised?" Muhammad asked, his voice sounding alarmed.

Mother turned to Father for an answer. He gave none, other than saying it was something that the great prophet

Abraham had done with his sons, Ishmael and Isaac. Honoring Abraham, the Muslims and Jews circumcise their boys.

To spread the word about the upcoming celebration, my parents decided to take us on a trip to the villages where many of our relatives lived. The nickname for all the villages was *balad*, place of origin, because here people lived a traditional life, unlike ours in the city. They knew one another so well that every house, orchard, and even water well had a name to indicate its owner.

For me and my brothers, going to the *balad* meant having lots of fun. There we would eat all kinds of fruits right from the trees, tie a rope on a pear tree and swing, and ride donkeys or horses if someone helped us climb up on their backs. And I would make bracelets for my sister and myself by stringing threads or thin metal wire through green acorns. The date for the circumcision was set for the Friday after we returned from our visit.

On the day of the trip, we woke up earlier than our parents, fed the goats and chickens, filled the grain and water cans to the rim, and impatiently waited outside for Father and Mother to join us. I loved seeing Grandma Fatima because everyone always said that I looked like her. She was strong and beautiful. Straight as a pillar, she could balance a jar of water on her head and walk for a mile without losing a drop.

"Do you think the house will be safe with no one in it?" Mother wondered out loud. She was worried that if some soldiers came during the day and noticed we were gone, they might take over the house as a hiding place for their training, trample the garden, or use the water supply and leave its lid open. If they came, no one would see them because our house stood alone. But there was not much we could do to protect it except lock the big front door and close the metal shutters. So we set out on our journey.

We took the bus from Ramallah to the town of Beit Hanina. "Sit quietly," Mother instructed. But I liked to turn my head and gaze at the girls who were, like me, dressed in clean, new, and colorful clothes. We all shook our feet in delight at our new shoes and looked at one another's hair ribbons, white socks, and especially our tin or plastic necklaces and rings. The windows in the bus were open to the hot breeze and road dust. And the bus stopped many times to pick up and drop off passengers.

At the Beit Hanina junction, we got off and waited for the bus that would take us to Nabi Samuel, the village where Father was born. As always, while we waited at that junction, he bought us ice cream from Mufid's shop, and Mother pointed to a two-story house on the main Beit Hanina–Jerusalem road and told me it was where I was born. "Dar Thehaibeh," she would say, remembering the name of the woman who owned the house. Seeing that house always made me happy.

In no time, we were on our way to Nabi Samuel. The village sat on top of a sharply rising hill preceded by many smaller ones. The old bus climbed slowly, and as the driver negotiated the gears, gas, and gravity, it felt as though at any moment it would roll backward. Then, reaching the top of a hill, it hiccuped forward, and I gripped my seat and prayed.

The bus raced down the other side, faster than either the driver or I wanted it to.

Nabi Samuel is named after the ancient prophet Samuel, who is believed to be buried there. A mosque honoring him is built on the highest point of the hill. Nabi Samuel seemed to have only a few homes; Father told us most of the people who used to live there, many of them our relatives, left because of the wars. But he knew the names of most Samuelis, whether they were living there or not. He could climb up and down the genealogical tree of Nabi Samuel the way my brothers and I climbed the fig tree next to our house. He told us many stories about our aunts, uncles, and dozens of cousins whom we had never met.

When the bus had come as close as it could to the village, we got off. As we walked the rest of the way, I lifted my eyes to the minaret that split the sky like the body of a bird between its two wings. The hot wind whistled faintly as it ebbed and flowed. It felt as though the trees were whispering secrets.

Aunt Rasmeyyah, Father's older sister, saw us from afar and hurried to meet us. Her sons followed. After kisses, embraces, and exclamations about how much we had grown, Father took my brothers and me for a walk.

First we went to the mosque. Only yards from the entrance, on the right side, we stood by the graves of Grandpa Hussein and Grandma Sarah, Father's parents. We said a prayer for their souls. They both had died before I was born. Their graves were marked with white stones that formed two necklaces around them. "Was Grandma Sarah pretty?" I asked my father. He said she was short and thin. Her eyes were brown and almond-shaped like a deer's, and she had a sweet smile. Standing by Grandma Sarah's grave, I said *Marhabah*, hello, and spoke to her as though she were standing with us. "My brothers did so well in school this year," I let her know.

I followed my father and my brothers up the minaret's spiral staircase. Only one person at a time could fit on the tiny steps. Bending through a low door, I walked out to find myself standing on a narrow balcony that surrounded the minaret like a bracelet. We stood as far away from the edge as we could, gluing our bodies to the minaret. When we touched the rail, it shook. I knew the balcony was not meant to hold more than one person. But each time we visited Nabi Samuel, my father wanted us to see the magnificent beauty of the land stretching in all directions, just as he had done a long time ago when he was a child.

Birds flew onto dancing treetops below me, and many distant towns flickered on the bright horizon, each with a minaret that pointed to the sky like a pencil pointing to a page. Vehicles that shone in the hot sun as they passed through Beit Hanina on the Ramallah-Jerusalem road appeared so small I felt I could pick up many of them in one hand and put them all in my pocket. Maha would be excited to see them.

"Do you know that a long time ago a man fell from this minaret but was not harmed?" Father mused.

We were astonished, for the minaret was so high. "How?" we all asked at once.

"He fell onto the back of a donkey," Father said. "And afterward, the donkey took the man home."

"Like a taxi?" we all asked, and laughed.

But Father said that he believed the story, and that God could make anything happen, God could have sent the donkey to this man the way He sent the ram to save the prophet Abraham's son, as the story in the Qur'an says.

I thought about God. I did not know who He really was because each time I asked about Him, who His parents were and what He looked like, my father said that no one knew what God looked like. But that He created all things.

"Who created God?" I then asked.

"No one" was my father's usual answer. "People's minds are too simple to grasp the endless nature of God," he would add.

Looking down from the tall minaret, I thought God must be kind to send a ram to save a boy and a donkey to save someone falling from a minaret. Then I remembered Souma, my donkey friend at the shelter during the war. I imagined the donkey my father mentioned standing there under the minaret the way Souma had stood in the shelter after the war. Was he sent to save me? But Souma and I now were in different worlds. And he must have grown just as I had. Would I recognize him if I saw him? Would he recognize me?

As we ate the feast Aunt Rasmeyyah prepared for us, many people came to say hello, and my parents invited them to the circumcision celebration we would be having in ten days. They looked at my brothers, patted them on the shoulders, and said that circumcision turned boys into men.

Before leaving Nabi Samuel, we visited the fields Father owned on one side of the village. He had bartered with someone to care for them, and now the land had trees with juicy yellow and purple plums, olive trees full of fruit, and grapevines that faced the sun all day and held grapes that had quickly ripened. Each field had a name, as though it were a person or a town. The flat field at the bottom of a hill was named Thaher Emran, Back of Emran, because it looked like the back of a man lying on his belly. Thaher Emran was planted with wheat. The golden seed braids waved like hands urging me to come nearer. The tender tops against my hand felt like long eyelashes.

Father then led us to a sunflower field with stalks taller than my brothers and me, even taller than him. I disappeared under a yellow sky of petals and discs. Scarecrows wearing jackets and hats and looking like dancing men flailed in the wind in many places. The daring crows stood right on the scarecrows' heads.

Before we left, my father found an abandoned soldier's helmet. A bullet had gone through it. Water had settled inside and caused it to rust. He buried the helmet in a little grave and said a blessing for the soul that might have been lost from the bullet.

Looking out at the red fields of Nabi Samuel, Father seemed sad. Many people had been saying that much of the land in Palestinian cities, towns, and villages would soon be confiscated by the Israeli government. He picked up a handful of the dry, red soil, then held it and stared at it for a long time.

In the afternoon we caught the bus once again and set out for Beit Iksa, the valley town below Nabi Samuel where both Grandma Fatima and Great-Grandma Jamila lived. The houses in Beit Iksa clustered around the only street in the village. The rest of the land was covered with orchards—almond, fig, apple, plum, pear—as well as vineyards. A giant eucalyptus tree and a water well, Bir El-Shami, marked the ramp that led to a higher field ending with Grandma Fatima's home.

Before we arrived in Beit Iksa, Mother reminded us not to cause any trouble for our grandmas, and to take only one piece of candy if offered. She had a silent code to communicate with us when we were visiting people or had guests visiting us. If she bit her lips, that meant "Stop talking." If she opened her eyes wide and glared at us, it meant "I see you and you must stop what you're doing immediately." She had many special eye movements, facial expressions, and finger gestures that asked us to eat, stop eating, sit, leave the room, or go find Father when needed. Most of all, before we visited Beit Iksa, Mother warned that we should stay away from the well, Bir El-Shami.

Like all the women in Beit Iksa, Grandma Fatima wore a long black dress embroidered with green, white, red, and pink flowers. When I asked her why she always wore the

same style dress, she said that Palestinian women had embroidered their dresses with these flowers for hundreds of
years. You could tell which town a woman was from by the
colors and style of flowers embroidered on her dress.
Grandma strapped a wide belt around her thin waist and
covered her long braids with a white scarf.

Her house had one room. She slept in one corner,
cooked and cleaned in another, had a cupboard and a closet
in the third. In the fourth were cushions where she and her
guests sat to visit. The windows were old and the screens
were rusted. But the breeze that came in and out with a
fresh orchard fragrance made the room feel new and beautiful.

The treats Grandma baked in her mud-and-stone
hearth were safe in a basket that hung from the ceiling,
where ants could not get at them. Our eyes immediately
went to the basket, and she smiled, reached up, took out
some of the anise cookies she often baked, and gave them to
us with tea.

Grandma worked all day caring for the land she lived on
and also for the orchards she'd adopted. She said she missed
her family's orchards in Kharrouba, the village from which
she, Grandpa Hammoudeh, Mother, and her siblings had
fled, along with all the other villagers, in the war of 1948.
But Grandma still kept the key to her old house there and
hung it on the wall where she could see it every day.

Grandma loved trees with all her heart, perhaps the way
I loved Zuraiqee. "They are part of my family," she assured

me. And she was right. Apple, pear, fig, sumac, apricot, almond, and peach trees stood within yards of her door and
seemed healthy and well cared for.

"Are these animals or fruits?" I would ask her, rubbing
my skin against the fur of peaches.

"Neither," she would reply with a laugh. "They are children." And she would dig her teeth into one to tease me,
making me laugh, too. She also kept chickens and rabbits.
The pigeons she raised lined the edges of her roof like store
awnings.

But the main member of Grandma's family was her own
mother, Great-Grandma Jamila. She lived in a separate
house, a few minutes away. Like many grandmas, Great-
Grandma Jamila had tattoos that adorned the backs of her
hands, her chin, and her forehead. She walked bent over and
was as wrinkled as a newborn baby. She slept as often as a
baby, too. When my brothers and I woke her up by playing
too loudly, she called for us to come inside to see her. We
did, sitting at the foot of her bed and then jumping on it as
though it were a trampoline. She was too frail for our tumbling, but she let us go on anyway, smiling a toothless smile,
her large eyes, the unending blue of a summer sky, sparkling
with pleasure.

Mother, holding the hand of my sister, soon joined us in
Great-Grandma Jamila's house. She announced that Father
had gone to the center of the village to invite relatives and
friends to the circumcision. Then she asked that we go outside and play.

My brothers and I knew that Mother would soon be

busy talking with Great-Grandma. No one would be watching us. So, against our parents' ongoing warnings to stay away from Bir El-Shami, the three of us agreed to sneak a look.

Bir El-Shami was so deep it never dried up the way other wells did. A fresh spring fed it when the rain stopped. It had a small opening but no cover. A black rubber bucket tied to a long rope lay beside it. Remembering Mother's words—that one's head is heavier than one realizes—we stretched our bodies on the ground before looking down into the well.

The liquid mirror inside reflected our faces. We called out one another's names; the echoes returned to us as though our voices had grown older than we were. We dropped tiny pebbles into the well. The water blinked like an eye, ripples spreading out like leaves of a giant cabbage.

Then, suddenly, Mother's voice reached us. "Where are the children?" she shouted. There was no answer. But we knew that soon she would discover us and chase us away from the water. We dangled our heads as low as we could, our bodies feeling lighter, our heads heavier and heavier.

Mother's voice came closer, calling out our names. But the water called to us even more loudly. We lay silent, our minds spread into two worlds, until suddenly Mother's steps were right beside us. Trembling with anxiety, we seemed to lose our balance. Unsure what would follow, we held on to the edge of the well, continuing to gaze into the water. Now I was afraid and wanted to cry. When Mother finally spoke to us, it was in a strange, quiet voice. She begged us to remain still. We obeyed. And then she helped us move away from the edge to safety.

Trailing behind Mother, we whispered to one another, trying to capture in words the feeling we'd had while staring into the water. But there were no words. Only silence could express it.

Mother was so grateful we hadn't fallen into Bir El-Shami that instead of scolding and hitting us she reached out and drew us to her—holding us tight. We no longer needed her warnings that many people had fallen into and died in wells. Now we saw the danger.

Circumcision

Zuraiq seemed to sense something strange as Father walked toward him. He leapt, stood far away amid the rocks, and looked ready to run farther. Had he overheard the news my parents had announced just minutes ago—that he would be killed for the circumcision feast?

"No!" my brothers and I had shouted at once. "You promised to keep him for us. You promised," we reminded our father.

We bombarded him with questions, pummeling him about not keeping his word. "I did," he insisted. "I did not sell Zuraiq to anyone." He protested that he could not afford to buy all the necessities for the feast and the celebration. But the feast, the celebration, and the circumcision meant nothing in comparison to Zuraiq. He was part of our family.

"You must say goodbye to Zuraiq and bring him to the shed," Father instructed. He knew we were the only ones Zuraiq would listen to.

We looked at one another and then, without a word, ran fast and furiously toward Zuraiq, yelling: "Flee! Forever! Never come back to the knife that awaits you." But Zuraiq must have thought we were playing. He stepped nimbly toward us, his ears flapping against his cheeks as he shook his head and brushed against our open hands.

"Go!" I begged Zuraiq to save himself. Rushing ahead of him, my brothers hoped he would follow them. And I ran after Zuraiq to make sure he kept moving. When we were far away from the house, the three of us suddenly reversed direction, charged away from Zuraiq, and threw pebbles at him. But that did not discourage him from running after us as though an invisible string existed between him and us. It became clear that it was impossible for us to make Zuraiq flee. Our only hope was to make our father change his mind.

Standing apart, we shouted that we wouldn't come home until he assured us he would not kill Zuraiq. Throwing his arms up in the air in agitation, he laughed, then turned to Mother. "They must think they're the children of a king if they believe we can afford to keep a goat as a pet for all its life."

"But you're the one who promised them," she chastised.

"I wanted them to be happy, if only for a while," he pleaded. "My own dad would never have let me keep a goat as a pet, even for a day." He picked up a pebble and threw it off into the distance. My brothers and I stood, crossing our arms against our chests, hoping our parents would decide in favor of Zuraiq's life.

"I will not kill him," Father suddenly announced. We leapt up in delight, but we were not going to take a chance in case he was deceiving us.

"Yamma, can you assure us he won't kill him?" Basel shouted.

"I assure you," she replied. So we ran back into the house cheering, with Zuraiq close behind us.

But the moment Zuraiq was within our father's reach, he grabbed him and put a leash around his neck. He led him out, locked the door, and ordered us to stay inside. We ran to the window. "Why?" we exploded. Father had no answer. He only looked away. Now we realized that we had been tricked.

"Listen," Mother said, turning to us sternly. "The circumcision date cannot be changed, and before we know it many people will be here for the celebration."

So this was Zuraiq's last hour? I could not imagine losing him. I felt he loved me more than anyone else. Hitting the wall with my fists and crying at the top of my lungs, I knew I should do something to help him. "Can you keep him alive one more day? I will do all the chores you want," I bargained with Mother. But her eyes said that it was no use.

When she turned to go outside, my brothers and I

begged her to let us say goodbye to Zuraiq and be with him as he died. Wagging her finger to warn us against disrupting, she opened the door.

We walked to Zuraiq silently, astonished at what we knew would happen in moments. We held his face and kissed him, told him that we loved him, and heard him for the last time bleat his love back to us. Holding hands tightly, we stood, backs against the wall.

Father tied Zuraiq's legs with short ropes, turned him upside down, read prayers over him, and, with Mother's help, severed the head from the body. Blood spurted everywhere. We dropped to the ground, weeping.

"I am sorry I ever made that promise," Father said. He cursed himself for having done it. But his apology did not change our loss one bit.

Zuraiq's body hung from a tree for hours as Father slowly skinned him. The mother goat, who was locked in the shed, had not seen her son's slaughter, but she hit her horns hard against the door. When she was let out, her eyes were wide and red like wounds. She stretched her chest tight like a bow, raised her head up, and screamed her grief into the sky for hours. I wished I could scream my own pain the way she did.

After skinning Zuraiq, Father ripped open the body. Mother cleaned the intestines, later to be cooked with spices and rice. She set aside the heart, and I held it, a tremble running through my body. I couldn't stop crying.

Mother packed Zuraiq's skin with salt and set it in the

sun to dry. It would make a rug or a winter cover—at least that part of Zuraiq would stay with us for years.

On the day of the circumcision, Grandma Fatima and the other women who came early to help Mother scrubbed the floor tiles and window glass till they squeaked like birds under their hands. They hung red, orange, and yellow balloons and shiny paper lanterns from the ceiling. They lined up dozens of borrowed chairs in our front yard.

Sitting on top of the cupboard were baskets filled with pieces of candy glittering in silver and gold wrappers like distant stars. Once the circumcision was completed, Mother would hand me the baskets. It would be my job to make certain every person present got a handful of candy.

The women made *mansaf*, the customary meal served at weddings and circumcision celebrations. On a large tray called *seder*, they spread fresh flatbread, layered with yellow saffron rice. They soaked the rice and bread with *jameed* yogurt, then topped it all with meat, pine nuts, and almonds.

Our Nabi Samuel and Beit Iksa relatives, other relatives who lived in Jerusalem, Father's co-workers and friends, Mother's friends and clients all began arriving at our home. The old men wore long traditional garments resembling dresses and covered their heads with black-and-white *hatta* scarves.

The women lined their eyes with dark kohl; some painted their lips and nails, and all of them wore black dresses colorfully embroidered with endless stitches, each the size of a sugar granule. It had taken Grandma months of work to embroider hers. The women compared the time it took them to complete a dress. They also compared the thickness and artistry of their golden dowry bracelets and jewels. The wealthier women had gold bracelets covering their arms from wrist to elbow. Mother owned only six bracelets, one pair of earrings, and a necklace.

The moment each woman guest arrived in the yard, and before she reached the door, she ululated, making a loud trilling sound, to announce that she shared our joy. Women already inside the house replied to the newcomer with similar cheers, and their sounds merged into a thundering song that reached up to the clouds.

When most of the guests had arrived, a man in the garden beat a drum, calling everyone to dance. Men and women raised their hands in the air, waved handkerchiefs, snapped their fingers as they tapped the ground, then stomped with their feet. They swayed their shoulders with delight, moving left and right in a circle.

Young children flooded to the center and danced till they were exhausted, only to get up and dance again. Maha was with them, happily running in and out of the circle like a baby clown. I leaned against the door, one moment looking at the dance circle, the next closely watching my brothers.

They were inside the house, trying every chance they got to charge toward the door. They begged to go outside for a moment, but the growing crowd guarded them lest they disappear before the arrival of the man who would circumcise them. What was going to happen? No one would explain anything to me. Confused, I knew I would understand only after the circumcision was done.

Then, suddenly, a voice from outside rose above the crowd. "Abu Qazem has arrived." The dance circle now became like a mad hive, and the songs sharpened.

Abu Qazem walked in a hurry, carrying a black leather briefcase. Everyone greeted him cheerfully. Father met him with a welcoming handshake, and led him to my brothers. I followed them as the trilling intensified, becoming one long siren call. Seeing Abu Qazem, my brothers kicked and pushed with all their might, trying to get out of the house. But the crowd blocked their path.

Muhammad was taken aside in order not to see while men pinned down Basel and removed his clothes. Basel screamed for help. I was stunned. Did they want to harm him? I shouted that they must stop, but Grandma quickly reached over and closed my mouth. I bit her hand.

The men pushed down on Basel's chest to make certain he could not get free or see what was about to happen. But I was seeing for him. Now that he was no longer able to make a noise, his mouth frothed like a boiling pot of milk on a stove.

The women joined in singing high rounds of praise.

> *The circumcised boy,*
> *His precious tears are*
> *Soaking his sleeves.*
> *Hand him to his mother.*

The circumcised boy,
His precious tears
Are a string of pearls.
Hand him to his father.

But Father and Mother were watching as Abu Qazem took out a steel rod. He used it to measure the length of foreskin that he was going to snip off. While carefully working his scissors, Abu Qazem commended Basel for his courage in enduring the pain of this ancient ritual. "Enduring pain makes you a man," he said.

Blood gushed into Abu Qazem's hands. He disguised the bleeding with Mercurochrome and swiftly wrapped it all with many layers of gauze.

He now turned around for Muhammad while half the crowd gathered to comfort Basel. I watched in shock as Muhammad was forced into circumcision.

"Give away the candy," Mother said, nudging me as Abu Qazem rose to leave the room. But I wanted to give candy only to Basel and Muhammad. I threw it all on them like confetti while relatives and guests leaned down to kiss them and put money under their tear-soaked pillows.

The food was served first to Abu Qazem; then everyone squatted around the large platters and ate. I could not eat anything, nor could my brothers, and by the end of the day, Zuraiq had disappeared.

In the days that followed, Basel and Muhammad put on loose dresses, washed their bodies with cool tea, and screamed in anguish each time they felt the urge to urinate.

They looked so helpless. They spoke mainly with each other, for they had shared the same loss.

I felt alone. Zuraiq was gone. And suddenly Basel and Muhammad seemed to have been taken from me, too.

School was going to start soon, and I would walk and take the bus with them every morning. But my excitement about going to school with my brothers had dimmed. Everything seemed different now.

Jalazone Girls' School

As the Singer sewing machine chugged up and down creating stitches in my blue-and-white elementary school uniform, I wondered why my brothers did not wear uniforms to school. Mother said that I would wear this dress with a pair of black stretch pants every school day. "How does a girl differ from a boy, Yamma?" I asked.

"The boys are like your father," she explained, keeping her eyes on the needle going up and down. "And you are like me."

I did not like this answer. I remembered Zuraiq. Mother was the one like my father. They had agreed to kill Zuraiq for the circumcision. My brothers and I were the ones who had tried to save him.

Foreseeing my stream of questions, Mother pulled out

the dress, cut the thread with her teeth, and placed a bundle of silver pins between her lips.

"Turn around," she instructed. She fitted the sleeves, attached them with the pins, then took the cloth back to the machine.

"Don't ask more questions," she begged. "They'll distract me and ruin your first school dress." She put another bundle of pins between her pursed lips. Each time I spoke, she pointed to them to show me that she could not reply.

I occupied myself by searching Mother's *Burda* fashion magazine for the faces of girls I liked. Would any of the Jalazone Camp schoolgirls I was going to meet in two days look like them? Would they become my friends?

In the final *Burda* pages, there were many pictures of stuffed animals. A giraffe, with its stretched-out neck, caught my fleeting glance. The neck curved like a slide. I wished Mother would make me one but dared not ask for it. She had said repeatedly that she did not have time to make stuffed toys. So I sculpted the chewing gum I had in my mouth into a miniature giraffe, fixing its long neck on a match, and handed it to her.

"You never give up!" she exclaimed, laughing.

Later that afternoon, Mother finished my dress. I put it on and dug my hands into the deep side pockets I had made sure she sewed into it. She had wanted to make square front pockets. But I wanted pants-style pockets that hung inside my dress like goat udders. I could hide big handfuls of salted sour green almonds and roasted chickpeas in them. No one would know. And on winter mornings, I could take two hot *rathef* stones from the oven after Mother had finished baking bread and put them in my pockets. They would warm my hands all the way to school.

With a proud grin, Mother looked on as I walked around the room. "You will be the best-dressed girl in the school," she promised. She pulled out a box with new white socks, a white collar that would fit around the neck of my dress, a white handkerchief to keep in my pocket, and white ribbons for my braids.

The next day, she made me a schoolbag. When she was done, a long giraffe head peeked from it. "I love you," she whispered. Her words startled me. That was the first time she had uttered such an expression of affection to me. "I want you to be first in your class," she continued. I did not know what that meant. "Sit quietly, listen to your teachers, and study with all your heart," she said, holding my hands tightly inside hers.

"Remember Alef and his family?" she asked. I nodded eagerly. "Your teacher will ask you about them."

Much of the schoolwork that my brothers had brought home over the previous year had included Alef and his family. I had memorized everything. I felt close now to all twenty-eight letters of the Arabic alphabet; I had adopted them as my own extended family.

The night before going to school I sat up and stared into the darkness. The giraffe was warm in my arms, and I thought about the long necklaces I was going to make, the cone paper hats, and the safety pins I was going to turn into earrings for her. And I thought about Mother's words. Would she still love me if I did not fulfill her wish? I tiptoed over to my school dress and stroked it for a long time. I thought of a classroom with an endless chalkboard where I would be first—in school and in my mother's heart.

The next morning my brothers, who had healed from their circumcisions, were happy that I was going to school with them. They told me over and over that if I needed anything they would be just a couple of minutes away.

Father gave each of us an allowance. And, like my brothers, I now carried my water bottle on one shoulder and my bag on the other. All our family took the bus toward the Jalazone Camp.

Only minutes from the bus junction, my brothers pointed to a long building, many times larger than our home and all of the Mahasreh houses put together. "That's the station where the soldiers who train around our house come from," Basel declared.

"And where the searchlights originate," Father pointed out.

Somehow, the big building reminded me of the hospital in Jordan I had gone to after the war, and I did not want to get close to it. In and out of the barbed-wire-fenced lot surrounding this army center, Land Rovers stopped and started, entered and departed, antennas shooting like metal sugarcanes from their rooftops. Soldiers walked here and there, all dressed in khaki. At the entrance to the center fluttered a large blue-and-white flag like the one the Israeli soldiers carried when they came to train by our home.

Shortly after passing the military area, we got off on the Nablus-Ramallah road that separated the UN girls' and boys' schools for refugee children. The boys' school stood to the right, hidden behind a huge wall. My father and my brothers disappeared inside.

Mother, Maha, and I went to the girls' school, on the left. From the street, I saw the many windows and the playground. The school's wall was low, "because, unlike boys, most girls don't climb over walls," Mother explained. But I knew that I could climb over the wall if I wanted to.

The principal, whose name was Sitt Samira, seemed much older than Mother. She had hair combed to the sides of her head like two wings. She did not smile as she led us to her tiny room flooded by morning light. We sat down in three seats that were lined up in front of her desk. Sitt Samira and Mother spoke about me as I rocked myself on the chair. I wanted to get up and touch the things in the room, but I knew that if I upset the principal I might not be accepted as a new student.

Mother praised me, but the principal dismissed her comments and said that my behavior would be observed during the year. "Side by side with learning," she said, as she took down the information needed to register me, "we emphasize cleanliness. If your daughter is not clean on any day, she will be punished or returned home."

"I bathe her once a week," Mother boasted.

"That's sufficient only if it keeps her head free of lice and fleas," the principal replied. She commented that many camp families were unable to keep their children clean because of poverty, lack of water, and shortage of space. "But we must require cleanliness," she emphasized, "especially from the girls."

Mother held my hand as we walked behind the principal across a square playground to the room where the first grade met all day. The principal knocked at the door. And— to my great surprise—the teacher who opened it had blond hair and blue eyes, just like a grownup *Burda* girl!

We entered, and everyone in the class was asked to stand up. "Lilian, this is your thirty-sixth student," the principal said to the teacher while pointing at me.

"Remember what I told you," Mother urgently reminded me for the last time, before she left with Maha.

Girls were lined up behind their desks from wall to wall. Lilian gave me a little smile and then said that I must sit in the back because I was taller than most girls. If tall girls sat in the front, shorter ones would not be able to see the board.

Everyone looked back for a moment to see where I would sit, then turned away to face Lilian. "Put up your hand if you want to speak or answer a question," she said, smiling again.

The white ribbons on all the heads appeared like a field of cyclamens before me. They blocked a full view of Lilian, whom I instantly liked because she smiled as she uttered every word. When she said she would teach us the alphabet and then picked up a piece of chalk and wrote Alef on the board, I raised my hand and called out Alef's name. When she wrote Ba and Ta, I did the same.

Surprised, Lilian came to the back of the room and handed me the first-grade reading book. She opened the pages and asked me to read. I knew every letter and every word. She quickly pulled my chair from the back of the room and set it at the edge of the classroom, closest to hers.

Lilian wrote on the board and had us repeat the letters and words after her. When we were to write in our copybooks, she taught me first, then asked me to make sure the other girls wrote the letters and words correctly. And so, at the age of six, I moved from seat to seat to help teach my classmates.

At home, I played school and pretended that I was Lilian. I did not hit anyone in my classroom or scold them. I drew stars in their imaginary notebooks. I praised them and asked everyone to clap after anyone read a letter or a word correctly. The ones who made mistakes were given as many chances as they needed to get it right, and then everyone clapped. My sister did not want to sit in the pretend class, but she helped in the clapping. And I told her over and over how kind and pretty Lilian was.

In Lilian's class or at the thought of her, I felt strong, as though I had become a grownup. But outside her class, many things still frightened and confused me.

Six Fingers

Every morning at Jalazone Elementary we lined up in the square playground and recited in unison "Surat Al-Fatihah," the opening chapter of the Qur'an. I knew this short chapter by heart and looked forward to the group reading. Its words had a fresh taste when spoken out loud and made me feel that I belonged with the Jalazone girls the way a drop of water belongs in the rain.

The river of our voices often reminded me of the soldiers near my house. They chanted, too. But unlike the schoolgirls who stood in the playground, the soldiers stomped and marched. I wondered if they were praying. Were they like us—daily asking God to show them the right path?

My morning excitement about "Surat Al-Fatihah" was interrupted daily by having to drink UNRWA milk. When ordered to do so by teachers, I untied the plastic cup I kept tied to my belt and waited for my turn. When it came, I watched the milk fill the cup as though it were liquid pain. It was nauseating. It tasted nothing like the milk our goat gave us. I tried to spill the milk somewhere when my teachers blinked, or give it to one of the girls from another class who did not mind the taste. She was much larger than me. And I knew that it was from all the morning milk other girls could not drink but she could.

Cod liver oil pills followed. "Don't chew the pills, and you won't taste the oil," girls reminded one another. Teachers watched like hawks to make sure we neither spilled the milk nor threw away the pills that had been donated by the United Nations.

For the cleanliness check, like everyone else, I held out my hands to show my nails. If they were long, I tried to bite them off before the teacher reached me, for fingers with long nails were slapped. An older student who accompanied the teacher then parted the hair of every girl. She raised each braid and looked closely at the nape of the neck. A slap followed if the teacher saw lice or fleas. The sound of that slap made me cringe, and I wished I could become invisible and disappear from the line.

The girls whose hair had lice or fleas stayed outside. A man with a DDT pesticide pump sprayed their heads as though the girls were plants. Already pale with embarrassment, the girls sprayed with the white powder looked like sad, old women.

"We're doing this to teach you cleanliness," the teacher

would say. "And in the higher classes you will be made to drop your pants and someone will sniff near you to make sure you have bathed," the student who was busy parting our hair would warn.

"But we have little water in the camp," the girls would whisper amid tears. Most of our teachers were not living in the camp. They came from Ramallah and other towns or villages. So how would they know?

I made sure Mother washed my clothes often. On the days she ignored me, I hung my school dress and stretch pants on the clothesline for the wind to shake them a thousand times. I sniffed them before I put them on. If they smelled of anything but soap, I argued with my mother that I should skip school that day, rather than be sent home in humiliation.

In the late afternoon sun, Mother and I sat in the backyard. I snuggled into her lap, and she groomed my hair. She searched it for lice and fleas. If she found one, she ran her nails along the hair and pulled it. Then she crushed the flea or louse between her nails. I twitched and screamed under her hands.

I felt Mother's breath in my ears as she warned me against sitting close to Jalazone girls. "The fleas jump from their heads to yours," she cautioned. "They might infect your hair." Mother insisted that I must never go to the camp or to the girls' homes.

But my classmates mainly came from the camp, and I wanted to know what their after-school clothes, their mothers, and their homes looked like. Nawal, whose father was the elder of the camp, said her family owned the only television in Jalazone. I had never seen a television and wanted to see theirs. Ilham, whose hair was longer than mine, also wanted me to visit her home. And I wanted to meet Nofaleyyah's mother, to see if she had six fingers like her daughter.

Nofaleyyah usually hid her sixth finger. But I noticed it when she took her hand out of her pocket and gripped the pencil to write the words I was to help her with. She held her breath and hovered over the page, pushing her pencil like a cane that supported her walk between the letters. Too short to tuck in with the rest of her fingers, her sixth stuck out slightly alongside her little finger. Her hand shook in frustration. If I waited and said nothing, she returned to her writing task. One day I asked Nofaleyyah if she would let me touch her sixth finger. Reluctantly, she did. "But don't tell anyone I let you do it," she begged. I promised. It was boneless, limp, and felt like dough.

Unlike me, Nofaleyyah was quiet and never joined in group play. But on some days at recess, she asked if I would walk around the school yard with her. I did. She got tired if she ran, she said. On these walks, she talked nonstop. I understood little of her stories because her voice was faint and she froze in fear if I asked her to repeat anything. Something in me worried about Nofaleyyah, because she was like an older person in the body of a little girl.

I liked the Jalazone school from the start. The girls taught me many games my brothers did not learn from the boys—hopscotch, handstands and even walking on my hands, jump rope, and cross-clapping that went along with songs. I also learned to fold paper into boats, animals, masks, birds, lanterns, and many other shapes. All the girls made friendship bracelets from plastic strings and colorful yarn, so I learned many ways of creating my own jewelry. And after watching several girls blowing bubbles with chewing gum, I could make bubbles the size of grapefruit. Some girls turned their eyelids inside out, and I learned to do that, too.

I liked the Jalazone school even more after Mother became pregnant. She walked slowly now and grew big like our goat. She spoke with agitation, demanding that I help with too many house chores. I wanted to study or go outside and play like my brothers. "They are boys!" she would shout. But I could never understand why a boy could play outside while a girl must stay in and work.

Mother no longer listened to me talk about school. She only asked quick questions. If she thought I lied in my answers, she opened my right hand, stuck her nose in it for a moment, and pretended that she could smell the truth. She also said that birds told her about me in my absence. I did not believe her. If they did, why hadn't they told her about Zuhair?

Big and tall, Zuhair lived at the end of the Mahasreh cluster of houses, closest to the Ramallah-Nablus Street. Everyone knew him as the teenage son of Abu Khalil. He had dropped out of school and often picked trouble with people. Every day after school, as I walked home from the bus stop, he would stare at me. At times he made frightening gestures with his tongue, lips, hands, and body.

One day he was leaning on the stone fence, arms crossed. His face had fresh fight cuts, and his eyes, round like wheels, followed every move I made. I was alone on the path with him. My brothers wouldn't be walking home for two more hours.

Thinking that I must run away from him, I flung myself across a row of thornbushes by the road. Zuhair leapt after me. He caught my arm, snatched away my schoolbag, and hung it from his shoulder. "If you pick cherries for me, I will return your bag and let you go," he bargained. Without hearing my reply, he dropped the bag to the ground, picked me up, and raised me to a branch.

The cherries were smooth like marbles and round like gum balls. There were many birds in the trees, and they saw me. I hoped they would fly and tell Mother.

When I started to pick the cherries, Zuhair began to roll up my dress. I opened my hands. The cherries tumbled everywhere. I fought to free myself. But Zuhair shook me and grunted that I must pick new cherries for him. I said no. When I felt him touch my skin, I dug my fingers toward his eyes and scratched. His hands pulled away as though from fire. He swayed left and right, then raised me as high as he could and threw me down.

Dirt flew up in a cloud as I hit the ground. I felt a curtain of darkness close in my head. A giant ache rippled through my body. Zuhair emptied my bag on the dirt and tossed it into the thornbushes. He threatened that if I told anyone he would kill me.

At home, I said that I had climbed a tree to pick cherries and had fallen from a branch. Mother said nothing. Then I knew for certain that the birds had not spoken to her.

The next day I announced that I no longer wanted to go to school unless I could wait and come home with my brothers. I did not want to walk home alone. Mother protested that I would be waiting for two hours until the boys' classes let out. But I persisted.

For many days I refused to go to school and refused to help at home. I hid under the bed from morning to evening until Mother changed her mind and said I could wait for my brothers.

Now Zuhair would not be able to touch me, and I had two extra hours a day that I could spend as I pleased. I was free again.

Elephant Boo

While waiting for my brothers after school, I snuck into the Jalazone Camp twice. Slipping down the steep road that led to the camp houses, I felt like I was walking to the bottom of the world. I had to lean back in order to keep my balance. A group of young boys were running up the steep street, then lying down and letting themselves roll like barrels.

Most of the houses of Jalazone were crowded shacks, some as small as the mudroom of our goat. Many had roofs made of uneven zinc or asbestos sheets held in place by rocks. They were jammed together on both sides of a tiny street that split the camp like a trickle of water. Spring-green spearmint, parsley, garlic, and scallion plants were planted in rusted cans by the doorways.

Many doors were open. Women asked me whose

daughter I was. I did not tell them. What if they knew Mother? If anyone told her I'd gone to the camp, she might keep me home from school. The camp women were busy with house chores. Their daughters all helped, and the look in their eyes told me how strange it was for them to see a girl wandering after school. But I was happy.

People in Jalazone seemed poorer than us and our Mahasreh neighbors. Women did most of their chores on the street. Water from laundry and dishwashing spilled between the feet of those who walked, for the camp had no sewage system. Bad smells wafted up from puddles of dirty water.

Many small children played in the street, running barefoot or even without clothes. Their faces were brown or gray with dirt. One child put his head out a window and screamed that he was hungry. His mother covered his mouth with her hand. "I fed him," she yelled from the same window to anyone who was listening. I knew many camp families did not have enough food. The flour and sugar *mu'an* rations donated by the UN for refugees came irregularly.

Going to Jalazone filled my heart with sadness. After only two trips, I no longer wanted to return. I also gave up on finding out whether Nofaleyyah's mother had six fingers like her daughter, or what the television in the camp elder's house looked like. Instead, I filled my hours of waiting by reading books I borrowed from my brothers or from my school. But because many of the stories reminded me of sad feelings I'd had, I retold them to myself as happier tales.

I knew what it felt like to be terrified and have to run

in the darkness of night and lose a shoe. So my Cinderella had her own magic wand and never had to worry about being missed. She would never lose her shoe.

I gave Leila Wa Al-Theeb, Little Red Riding Hood, a dragon friend to go with her to her grandmother's house so she would never have to feel like I did when Zuhair stopped me on my way home from school. When the wicked wolf saw the dragon's flaming breath, his jaw dropped so low that the swallowed grandma slid out safely on his tongue.

But the story that occupied my mind for the longest time, the story that I retold over and over, was about a baby elephant named Boo. He lived with his mother in faraway wild forests. Every day Boo and his mom searched for food, water, and safe places to rest and sleep. With their giant bodies and enormous ears, they stomped through the forests. Over time Boo's mother taught him how to be a good elephant. He learned quickly, and she was happy with him.

One day, Boo's mother told him that she was feeling ill and would soon die. She must walk to a distant place near a big body of water and lie there. Many dying elephants would lie by that body of water, which became what people called an elephant graveyard.

"Let us go," Boo's mother urged, nuzzling him with her trunk. Boo cried upon hearing his mother's words. He roared in anguish. Then they began their last journey together.

They walked side by side, and I walked with them through the winding roads of the forests. I knew that when

Boo's mother finally left him by the water and closed her eyes, he would feel what I had felt when I was separated four years ago from my family in the war. I wanted to be there for him, to comfort him and speak into his giant ear that he was not alone. He could hold my hand.

Boo's story made me worry about Mother. I became anxious that she might die during the day when I was away at school. I feared that the soldiers might harm her. I felt bad that I could not go home right after school. But it was too scary for me to risk walking alone with Zuhair on the road.

I also panicked about Mother at night. When she slept, I tiptoed in the darkness to where she lay. I put my hand close to her nose. I wanted to see if she was breathing and alive. Feeling her breath reassured me, but only momentarily. I wondered if she had died the second I walked away. I checked her breathing over and over for a long time until she woke up, agitated.

I continued until she asked me why I kept reaching for her nose and mouth. Whimpering, I told her. She said that she was not going to die soon. She also promised that she would not die without telling me first and saying goodbye the way baby elephant Boo's mother did with him. So I stopped checking on her breathing at night. But I never stopped feeling sad for Boo. Thinking of him walking back home motherless, tears rolling down his cheeks and tusks, I pulled the covers over my head and quietly cried with him until I fell asleep.

Mother gave birth shortly before the end of the school year. My father was especially happy with the new baby. He carried him back and forth across the room and cried tears of joy as he sang for him. I was most excited about the baby's tiny feet and hands. I kept putting my feet next to them to compare sizes. Maha wanted to carry the baby, but he was too heavy for her. Muhammad liked to kiss the baby's ears. But sometimes he bit the baby's earlobes and made him cry.

To celebrate the birth, Father handed me a big box of Silvana chocolates to give to my schoolmates and teachers. I ate half of the box on the way to school and shared the rest with the girls and teachers I liked. Grandma Fatima stayed with us and took care of Maha, Mother, and the new baby while my brothers and I were finishing school.

On the last day of the school year, we stood in the playground to receive our certificates. The principal talked about the importance of hard work and obeying the rules. *"Man jadda wajad,"* she said, meaning that those who persist shall achieve. Then she announced that she was going to call out the names of those who ranked first in their classes and that they would receive presents.

I knew Mother would love me more if I ranked first. But I did not know what to expect. What did it mean to rank first? I had done everything my teachers had asked me to do. But everyone else in my class had also done that.

The principal now smiled. A mound of colorful, shiny presents was on the table beside her. She began with the first grade. "Ibtisam Barakat," she called. I felt excited and a bit scared.

Lilian motioned that I should walk up and receive a purple package. When I did, the principal smiled and said something to me—perhaps a compliment, but I could not hear it because everyone was clapping.

Walking back to my place, I knew I wanted everyone in my class, especially Nofaleyyah, to receive a present. My classmates crowded around me, wanting to know what I got. I opened the wrapping before everyone to find an orange ball and a yellow pencil. They glittered like gold in the sun. I felt they were treasures.

Going home, I carried my certificate close to my chest the way Mother carried my baby brother. I placed it in her hands and showed her the presents. She walked slowly to her jewelry box, pulled out her only pair of golden earrings, and put them on my ears. I ran to the mirror to see what my first pair of earrings looked like. They sparkled like stars. And Mother's happy face sparkled, too. Now I felt that I had earned her love.

Home

Summer passed, erasing the last traces of wild-flowers and green grass. Migrating birds appeared as though barrels of confetti had been poured across the sky and swirled in endless formations. I waved to them. And soon it was time to return to school again. I was eager to be in the second grade. I had missed Lilian and all my classmates. I wanted to show off how long my hair had grown in only three months.

But the second grade was different from the first. And it had a different teacher. I wanted to be with Lilian. I would repeat the first grade if my teacher would let me. So I kept looking away from my teacher and out the window, searching for ways to be with Lilian.

In the morning, bending my knees and hiding my head, I pretended that I belonged in the line of first graders. But the teachers knew me, and one of them always reached in and pulled me out of the line. So during the day I asked to be excused and knocked at Lilian's door. I begged her to let me in, but she told me to go to the next room—the second grade. When she shut the door, I sat in front of it, crying.

Then Lilian and my new teacher talked. They agreed that because I often quickly finished my in-class work, then sat doing nothing, I could visit Lilian's class in my free time. But now, because my new teacher let me go to Lilian's class, I felt that she, too, was good, and I began to like her. Almost immediately I stopped wanting to leave the second grade and go to the first. But I continued to run to Lilian, to talk with her whenever I saw her during recess. And I continued to love her best.

That October I was planning to save a large piece of the cake Mother had promised to make for my birthday for Lilian. But only four days before my birthday, we heard terrible news and Mother canceled the cake. Father was first to hear it on the radio. It made him open his mouth wide in wordless anguish. He held his head between his hands as though the words that had entered his ears made his head too heavy to carry. "Jamal Abdel Nasser has died," he shrieked. "Now we are all orphans."

In the coming days, I learned that Abdel Nasser was the leader of Egypt. "He cared about all Arabs," my father lamented. Abdel Nasser had been trying hard to stop the fighting between the government of Jordan and the Palestinian freedom fighters we called *fedayeen* when he had a heart attack and died.

People in Ramallah mourned, gathering in large groups and carrying empty coffins to show the sadness of having lost the leader they loved most. Father walked in one of these funeral processions. And though he had never bought a newspaper because he always relied on our radio, when he came home that day he brought one with him. Abdel Nasser's picture was at the center of the front page.

Mother read every word out loud, punctuating each sentence with her tears. When she was finished, she carefully cut out the portrait of Nasser standing in a decorated military uniform. Under the photograph she wrote in the best form she could muster: *"Inna hurreyyata al-kalemah heya al-muqaddematu al-oula lel-deemuqrateyyah."* Freedom of the word is the first prelude to democracy. She had heard Nasser say this on the radio, and she repeated it often. Mother made a frame with cardboard, glue, and thread, and Nasser's photograph, with this sentence written underneath, was the only picture in our home.

When we heard recordings of Nasser's voice or speeches, we became silent as though we were hearing prayers. Father touched the radio gently and turned the volume up until Nasser's voice filled the world. Thumping songs, with tunes like elephant footsteps, followed. They shook the walls of my heart. I broke down sobbing, not knowing exactly why. A radio chant that wailed *"Nasser ya hurreyyah,"* describing Nasser himself as freedom, stuck in my mind like a rhyme. At the Jalazone school, teachers announced the loss by wearing black.

The death of Abdel Nasser was accompanied by increased military activity in our area. During the months that followed, I repeatedly heard sudden explosive noises from Israeli planes that forced me to run to hide. "They are breaking the sound barrier," Mother said. "It means they are flying faster than the speed of sound, faster than you can hear me speak." Then the planes flew high and needled into the sky that spread above them like a thin fabric. They dragged white smoke threads that thickened into clouds before disappearing. These planes stitched fear into my heart. What were the soldiers going to do next?

Other planes flew low, and I could see their big bodies, like moving buildings. They sounded as though they were right above our rooftops, and hearing them rekindled the feeling of war in me. When I heard them, I made certain I had my shoes on and kept an eye on my sister and baby brother. If a war started, I was going to make sure that the younger children were not forgotten.

Pressing his cheek against the radio set, grimacing in anger at the static that always intercepted the words, Father cursed, saying that we were living in the middle of a daily war. Where was it leading us? It seemed to him that the planes flying low above Ramallah were meant to keep us frightened. And we were.

But Mother was the most frightened. She kept her suitcase by the door. The sight of that suitcase struck horror in my heart. I worried that she might leave without taking us with her.

Everything reached a breaking point months later on a spring afternoon when two soldiers came to our door.

Thinking they wanted a drink of water, Mother impatiently pointed to the water room. But they laughed, walked to the well, then returned.

One of them pulled out his gun and stood away from the window to guard the door. The other threw kisses at Mother, hugged and touched his body up and down as he pointed to hers.

His gestures were similar to Zuhair's. Zuhair was Palestinian like us, and the soldiers were Israeli, but it seemed they wanted the same thing. I looked at Mother's face. She was pale and trembling. Before the soldier left, he made a circle with his hands, meaning that he would return on another day.

"There will be no other day," she promised. *"Khalas! Khalas!"* she announced when my father came home, tears filling her face. "This is the limit," she said, her voice firm with finality. Father did not argue. Though it was the middle of the school year and we would miss classes during the move, he quickly sold our house and found a place in the Irsaal area for us to move to. There, we would be surrounded by many other homes, and we would not have soldiers training near us.

I wept as we packed our belongings. Spreading sheets and blankets on the floor, we filled them with clothes, shoes, books, and kitchen items. We tied the blanket corners together into giant knots. I wrapped glass cups and plates inside blouses to protect them from breaking. The bullet inside the bed rolled against the metal as we swayed between steps, put the bed down for a rest, then started again. Father roped everything to the sides of the truck.

On the first trip, he took only Mother to help him unload our belongings into the new place. When we were done filling the truck again, our house had become as empty as the feeling I had in my heart. I built a *qantara* of seven flat stones by the door, the number of our family members. And I watered our garden for the last time with as much water as I could, in case no one would be there soon to care for it.

Sitting on a large rock facing the house as one faces a dying friend, my father picked up tiny pebbles from the ground and tossed them to the side. He raised his head and looked at the sky. "What have I done to deserve this sorrow?" he shouted. "I neither drink alcohol nor gamble, as you ordered. I don't even smoke," he pleaded with God. White clouds passed above him like angel caravans, perhaps carrying the complaints of others.

Mother locked the house. I wrapped my fingers around the window bars and looked into the emptiness. We had left nothing behind, but I still could see in my mind all of our things in their places. The brown cupboard standing with its screen doors open, the baby cot swinging like a pendulum, the Singer sewing machine pedal chugging up and down, pieces of cloth spread out on the tile floor.

I saw images of myself and my brothers reaching one more time for the Silvana chocolate box Mother always hid. Zuraiq's face appeared, then the sight of my brothers being circumcised, their mouths open with fear. I saw Mother handing me her only pair of gold earrings, and my sister and me as we banged cups on the table, drunk with the joy of the noise we created.

Outside, on the step in front of the locked door, my three-and-a-half-year-old self stood silently, screaming for my parents to wait for me. The feeling of that moment stung like fire in my heart.

Taking a final look around, I knew that this was the only place that would ever be home for me. And now I was leaving it and might never come back.

Mother's voice pulled me like a rope. She seemed cheerful and chattered about how our new home was in a large building that housed three other families and had a brick wall all around it. She wanted many neighbors.

I walked to the truck and climbed to the top of the pile of belongings, where my brothers were waiting. Father drove away slowly, and the distance between us and our home widened. We waved to the hill, the horizon, and the house, to the stone person, to the plants, and to the green door with the two windowpanes like eyes.

Then my father took a turn and the road closed like a final curtain behind us.

PART III

A Letter to Everyone

1981, Ramallah, West Bank

Like a bird flinging
Its freedom songs
Across the sky

The small girl
I once was
Sings out this story.

I see her smile.

I am midway from forgetting to remembering. I do not know how long it will take before I return to all of myself. Yes, an echo still warns: "Learn to forget." But I am past this checkpoint—I will never regret that I chose to remember.

The window into the past frames the new road before me like a postcard. I want to send it to all of my faraway pen pals. Now I can answer their questions about my childhood.

Dear everyone: Written on my heart, all that I lost—my shoes, a donkey friend, a city, the skin of my feet, a goat, my home, my childhood—shattered at the hands of history. But my eternal friend Alef helps me find the splinters of my life . . . and piece them back together.

A Song for Alef

Alef the letter
Is a refugee.
From paper
To paper
He knows
No home.

Alef the letter,
He is the shape
Of a key
To the postal box
Of memory.

Alef the letter
Sits in the front
Of the bus
Of alphabets
To see.
He sees war,
He looks above it.
He sees war,
He looks below it
And beyond it
To see peace.

Alef knows
That a thread
Of a story
Stitches together
A wound.

Alef the letter,
He's the shape
Of hope.
Like me,
A refugee.

For me,
My refuge.

Be kind, for everyone you meet is fighting a great battle.

—Philo of Alexandria

TO LEARN MORE

The following resources may be helpful starting points in exploring some of the larger issues related to *Tasting the Sky*.

The Flag of Childhood: Poems from the Middle East, selected by Naomi Shihab Nye (New York: Aladdin Paperbacks, 2002). These poems first appeared in a larger collection, *The Space Between Our Footsteps: Poems and Paintings from the Middle East* (New York: Simon & Schuster, 1998).

The sixty poems for young readers in this outstanding anthology transcend separations, silences, and barriers and bring the people of the Middle East—Iraqi, Saudi, Egyptian, Turkish, Israeli, Palestinian, and many others— together in a poetic homeland of openness, kindness, and beauty, under a borderless flag of childhood.

The Lemon Tree: An Arab, a Jew, and the Heart of the Middle East, by Sandy Tolan (New York: Bloomsbury, 2006).

This powerful narrative focuses on two families, one Israeli and one Palestinian, and the land, house, and lemon tree that unite and divide them. In a masterful weaving of historical and personal accounts, *The Lemon Tree* shows how the horrors of the Holocaust in Europe and colonialism in the Middle East eventually led to horrors in the Holy Land between Jews and Arabs. The current situation between Palestinians and Israelis is rooted, like a tree, in the turbulent layers of the historical soil that nourishes it. The interdependence of Palestinians and Israelis in their losses, realities, and dreams is a source of hardship as well as hope. This balanced and impressively documented book is a treasure.

Peace Begins Here: Palestinians and Israelis Listening to Each Other, by Thich Nhat Hanh (Berkeley, California: Parallax Press, 2005).

With its emphasis on nonviolence and compassion, this book is an inspiring step toward world-community building. It highlights many courageous personal accounts of Israelis and Palestinians who are seeking peace, within themselves and with one another. The book came out of ongoing Buddhist "peace retreats" that took place in Plum Village in France under the guidance of Nobel Peace Prize nominee Thich Nhat Hanh.

Promises, a film by Justine Shapiro, B. Z. Goldberg, and Carlos Bolado (http://www.promisesproject.org).

This film is a groundbreaking and well-balanced documentary about seven Palestinian and Israeli children between nine and twelve years old, living a short distance from one another yet existing in dramatically different worlds. *Promises* also explores the deeply moving moments when a few of the children cross the divide to reach for possible friends on the other side.

The study guide that accompanies *Promises* is an invaluable educational resource geared toward teachers working with middle and high school audiences. It includes teacher lesson plans that can be correlated to state standards for social studies, history, and language arts; creative activities; an excellent annotated list of related resources such as international newspapers, books, Web sites, and organizations; as well as contact information for peace groups.

Seeds of Peace (http://www.seedsofpeace.org).

A vibrant organization that aims to create peaceful, innovative, and cooperative connections among young people from the Middle East, Seeds of Peace has been expanding to include other areas such as the Balkans, South Asia, and Cyprus. Seeds of Peace started out in 1993 with forty-six Israeli, Palestinian, and Egyptian teenagers and now has a network of over 2,500 young people from twenty-five countries on four continents. At the Seeds of Peace international camp in Maine, teenagers build friendships, learn leadership skills, and engage in a wide variety of activities that foster conflict resolution, understanding, cooperation, and respect.

Three Wishes: Palestinian and Israeli Children Speak, by Deborah Ellis (Toronto: Groundwood Books, 2004).

This daring book brings together the voices of twenty Israeli and Palestinian children between the ages of eight and eighteen. These young people speak about how the Israeli-Palestinian conflict affects their lives. Sharing a wide range of experiences and viewpoints, they also express feelings, some raw and startling, others simple and ordinary. The book includes a brief historical overview of the Israeli-Palestinian conflict and an introductory profile of each of the young people that also provides context for some of the issues raised.

We Just Want to Live Here: A Palestinian Teenager, an Israeli Teenager—an Unlikely Friendship, by Amal Rifa'i and Odelia Ainbinder with Sylke Tempel (New York: St. Martin's Griffin, 2003).

This book offers an insightful and relevant account of correspondence between two eighteen-year-old girls, one Palestinian and one Israeli. The two girls met during an international exchange program but lost touch when they returned home to Jerusalem during the second Intifada. Two years later, in 2002, Middle East correspondent Sylke Tempel encouraged the teenagers to begin a conversation through letters to each other. During the months that followed, their candid personal exchanges opened crucial doors of understanding to each other's world. This moving book sheds much-needed light on the genuine concerns of both the girls and their peoples. It includes a short introduction by Sylke Tempel, a detailed chronology, and a glossary of terms.

GIVING BACK TO THE WORLD

Without the help of the United Nations Relief and Works Agency (www.unrwa.org), millions of other children and I would not have gone to school or learned to read, write, and use our pencils to clear a tiny path through the wreckage of refugee life, thereby plowing a plot of hope inside our hearts so that we could plant our dreams.

In writing Tasting the Sky *I give my story to the world in the hope that no others ever lose their home, and that the world would lend them a hand if they fell.*

I thank you:

Suzanne Fisher Staples
Naomi Shihab Nye
Frances Foster
Jennifer Armstrong
Saed Muhssin
Joan Drury
Virginia Duncan
Dan Nickerson
Victor Navasky
Kris Meilahn
Mike Markovits
Sally Seagull Foster
Sharif Elmusa
Patrick McClung
Tracy L. Barnett
Joan McElroy
Jane Franck
Allia Rahman
Melanie Kroupa, Sharon McBride,
and everyone at Farrar, Straus and Giroux
who helped to create this book.

And a special thank you
to the quiet city of Columbia, Missouri,
where it is possible to gently face oneself—
long enough to become friends,
a crucial element for world peace.

Photo courtesy of Michael J. Cooney, Oshkosh Rotary Club, 2015.

I begin most of my speaking engagements by singing in Arabic to bring my first language that I love into the room with me wherever I go. Singing also introduces the audience to a key element of Arab culture and creates a more open atmosphere. Music unites cultures, and only people who like us sing for us.

Sesame Treat Recipe

This is a treat that my father used to give me and my brothers. When I grew up I learned to make it, and now you can make it, too. It is simple, delicious, and nutritious.

Ingredients
1 cup of roasted sesame seeds
1 tablespoon honey
Spices or grated coconut flakes (optional)

Preparation
Spread the sesame seeds inside a skillet. Heat the skillet on a stove over medium setting, gently stirring the seeds nonstop for two to three minutes, until they are warm. Then remove the skillet from the stove. Add the honey and mix well until all the seeds are coated. (You will be surprised at how far a small amount of honey will spread.)

With a large spoon, scoop and place the sesame and honey mix on a large, flat plate or a baking sheet and let cool for three minutes, until the mixture becomes less sticky.

Then use a spatula to spread and smooth over the mix until it is flat with even thickness. Let cool for a few minutes until it is hardened. Sprinkle with grated coconut flakes or any spices you would like. Cut into small or large squares with a knife or a pizza cutter.

Serve and enjoy this treat from a Palestinian childhood.

Twelve Conversational Phrases in Arabic

✦

Nothing creates an opportunity for friendship better than speaking another person's language. Even using just one word can make someone feel more at home and open a window for cross-cultural learning.

To begin speaking Arabic, here are twelve phrases you can learn:

1. Marhabah. (Hello.)
2. Ahlan. (The reply to "Marhabah.")
3. Ismee _____. (My name is _____.)
4. Keef halak al-yawm? (How are you today? *spoken to a male*)
5. Keef halek al-yawm? (How are you today? *spoken to a female*)
6. Ana uheb _____. (I like, or I love _____.)
7. Ana la uheb _____. (I don't like, or I don't love _____.)
8. Ana ureed _____. (*formal request*) or Ana biddy _____. (*informal*) (I want _____.)
9. Ana la ureed _____. (*formal expression*) or Ana ma biddy _____. (*informal*) (I do not want _____.)
10. Assef. (Sorry. *spoken by a male*) Assefah. (Sorry. *spoken by a female*)
11. Shukran. (Thank you.)
12. Salam. (Peace. *Also can be used informally as "hello" or "good-bye."*)

GO FISH

IBTISAM BARAKAT

What do you want readers to remember about your books?

I want my readers to remember whatever helps them and whatever enriches their lives with beauty and heart and expands their possibilities. One college student sent me a letter and a photograph of her forearm with two lines from *Tasting the Sky* tattooed on her skin. That touched me deeply. So my readers also help me to remember why I write and give me new reasons to write. I thank them all—especially those who take a moment to tell me how my words affect them.

If you were a superhero, what would your superpower be?

Healing children's hearts from the promises made and not kept by adults. And making people of all ages remember their childhood joys and dreams and the excitement of discovery and simple living.

What's the best advice you have ever received about writing?

That writing is a relationship. If I bring love to it, invest in it, and nurture it generously, it grows and flourishes. If I neglect it, it does not flourish.

What advice do you wish someone had given you when you were younger?

That I have a compass in me and it knows my purpose, my dreams, my destination. If I ask it, it tells me where the right direction is at any moment. Also that there is an inner world for each person, and that each person needs to explore inwardly and outwardly to create a balance between the two worlds.

What is your favorite word?

Integrity. It is an "I" word like my first name. For me it has to do with whole numbers, integers that are not broken into fractions. I relate this word to understanding life and society. I see that the forces that break up a thing or person or a community or a society or the world into fractions and divide it decrease integrity, and what brings more wholeness increases integrity. The moral judgment commonly attached to this word often overlooks the beauty of the mathematical reasoning behind it.

Keep reading for an excerpt of the companion to *Tasting the Sky*, which tells the story of the author coming of age in Palestine.

Stone House

Grandmother Fatima has just arrived from her village in Jerusalem, at our new apartment on Radio Street, on the northern side of Ramallah in the West Bank. She is carrying her woven bamboo basket filled with green almonds. Grandma does not say whether she likes or dislikes our new place. When I ask her she says, "All that matters is that we are in the same country and I can visit you." Grandma then asks me to remind her how old I am, what school I go to now, and what grade I am in. I tell her that I am seven and a half years old, still go to the United Nations Relief and Works Agency (UNRWA) Jalazone Girls' School, and will soon complete the second grade. I am about to show her that I can write my name and many other words, but I stop when I remember that she has never gone to school and cannot read or write hers.

Mother and Grandma go to the kitchen. I follow them

quietly, hoping to listen in on their conversation and learn about the strange world of grown-ups and its many surprises—marriages, money, deaths, and whispered problems about relationships.

Today Grandma is speaking about Aunt Amina, one of Mother's two sisters. Aunt Amina lives in Amman, Jordan. She and her husband, Nimer, have ten daughters and no sons, and he insists he wants a boy to carry his name. Nimer is a professor at a university. Everyone in our family calls him *mitaallem*, educated.

Grandma is worried about Aunt Amina's safety because seven months ago, in the middle of September 1970, thousands of Palestinians living in Jordan were killed when the fedayeen, the Palestinian freedom fighters, and the Jordanian army had one of their worst battles. The hostilities began even before September and haven't ended yet.

The fedayeen wanted to gain more political and military control inside Jordan in order to fight Israel from the Jordanian border so they could take back Palestine from Israel and return to the homes and cities they lost in the war of 1948 that led to the *Nakba*, Catastrophe, and then the Six-Day War that led to the *Naksa*, Setback, of 1967.

The fedayeen hoped that Jordan would help them in their fight against Israel. But the Jordanian leaders did not want the fedayeen to organize non-Jordanian military groups inside their country, so they fought and the Jordanian army won after a massacre of Palestinians so grim that the month of Ayloul is now called Ayloul Al Aswad, Black September. Those words make me think of a whole month without the sun rising once.

"Every time I pray, I leave on the prayer rug big questions that I believe only Allah can answer," Grandma says. "They are about the future and what will happen in this woeful Holy Land. But even after I pray, the questions are still there in my mind and in the world." She raises her arms to the sky pleading: *"La-aimta ya rab?"* Dear God, until when?

"Nothing in our lives is predictable, but let's not despair," Mother says.

Mother and Grandma begin to exchange happier family stories, entangled with names, nicknames, and half events. They finish each other's sentences and I try to understand and arrange in my mind the names of my relatives, especially those I have not met because they live in other countries, or those who have died but continue to live in these stories as I learn new pieces of how they fit into our family history.

When Grandma gets up to leave, I pick up her basket and walk with her to the bus stop near the giant radio tower with the frightening skull-shaped high-voltage danger signs that order people to stay away. Radio Street is named after this broadcast tower, which was built by the British forces when they ruled over Palestine after World War I. Perhaps from this day on, every time Grandma Fatima listens to a radio program, she will think of us.

When the bus leaves, carrying Grandma with it, I try to guess how she feels about our new apartment. I hope she disliked it, because ever since we moved here, one month ago, I have been trying to convince myself to like it, but in my heart I do not.

Most of me still lives at the stone house we left behind on top of a hill near Nablus Road on the northeastern side of Ramallah. There, I often hid behind big rocks or lay on them, feeling their warm backs against my own. I picked colorful wildflowers and crushed them to use as finger paint on the rocks. I played with turtles on the gravel road, removing obstacles from their paths, sometimes carrying them and running so they would reach their homes faster. I also liked to place bread crumbs on their backs for them to take to their children.

I think about that house every day, but it is no longer made of stone. Now it is made of memories—hours spent watching migrating birds in the sky, waiting for dinner, for Mother to come home after shopping trips, or for Father to come home from driving his truck.

I remember the toys my older brothers created: cars they built from thin colorful electrical wires; skateboards constructed from wooden vegetable boxes fixed on ball bearings they got from abandoned car tires; kites made with bamboo stalks and newspaper glued together with bread dough; musical instruments shaped from rubber bands strung against a cooking pan; slingshots carved from tree branches; and origami rockets tied to strings and then to Mother's clothesline and left to fly all day.

I can also change my memories as I choose. The garden in front of the house now has magical plants that grow both fruits and vegetables. Rain never falls, except right into designated water containers or within the borders of the front garden. Sometimes a passing purple cloud rains sweet black grapes. We all open our mouths to catch and eat them.

My parents bought the stone house five years ago, when I was two and a half years old, right after the birth of my younger sister, Mona. And even though only my youngest brother, Samer, was born there, a year ago, and the rest of us children were born in different cities—Basel, who's ten and a half, in Jerusalem; Muhammad, who's nine and a half, in Jericho; Mona, who's five, in Al-Bireh; and I in Jerusalem—I feel as though all of us were born there.

We left the stone house once before, four years ago, on June 5, 1967, when the Six-Day War started. We had to run from shelter to shelter and from fear to fear as Israeli, Egyptian, Syrian, and Jordanian armies fought. The six days became one hundred and thirty-five days for us because it took that long before we could return to Ramallah with the help of the United Nations and the International Red Cross. At the end of the war Ramallah was occupied by Israel and we began to live as refugees in our own homes and on our own land, with no rights to travel to other countries and be assured that we could come back, no rights to cultivate most of the lands we owned, and no rights to build new homes or start new businesses without the permission of *al-hakem al-askari*, the Israeli military ruler. But when we returned and lived in the stone house again, that helped me to remember how I had felt before the war: happy and safe.

Then Israeli soldiers started to come daily to train on our hillside. We could see them outside our window as they set up camps surrounded by barbed wire. They ran drills and practiced shooting at cardboard cutouts shaped like people, leaving them with countless bullet holes that bled air.

My siblings and I found many ways to become less afraid of the soldiers, including climbing the barbed wire around their camps after they left for the day, playing hide-and-seek inside the trenches they had dug, gathering empty bullet shells, and peeking through the holes in the cardboard people—it was like looking through binoculars into a smaller world.

But then some soldiers began to knock on the door when Father was at work. They asked for a drink of water, even though they carried water bottles. They looked at Mother as though she was the water they wanted to drink. Each time, Mother pointed from the window to our well, which the soldiers could use to refill their bottles, then we pulled the curtains shut and made certain that our door was locked and pushed all the furniture we could gather against it. We watched the soldiers from the slits between the curtains.

We could no longer go outside, except after the army left for the evening. So my parents decided to leave the stone house forever. They sold it and searched for a different place for us to move to. We came here. I wish we hadn't, and that the Israeli soldiers had gone to train somewhere else instead.

This new house is a one-story white stone villa that looks like a giant ship sailing on a green grass sea. There is a small orchard and a hedge that surrounds everything like the edges of a huge box.

Our apartment is in the basement, so that we can be hidden from all eyes like rabbits in a burrow. Mother especially is happier underground, in this war-shelter-like place. But Father, although he says nothing about the move, appears sad. He was proud to own the house we lived in, proud of improving it as he liked. Here he cannot change anything, and there is no space for him to keep a goat and sing to it every evening like he did in the stone house. Singing helps Father feel happier.

Basel and Muhammad are content to run and play in a nearby meadow with other boys who gather for soccer games. But I continue to be afraid because the news on the radio speaks daily about death and fighting in many places. I do not know how far away the places they mention are from our house.

Father tries to help me overcome some of my anxious feelings. He explains that Vietnam is not nearby and the war there is not about us. Because Grandma's village in Jerusalem is called Beit Iksa—and dozens of other Palestinian villages begin with *Beit*—and because *nam* is also a word in Arabic, I had thought Vietnam was Beit Nam, and that its war was also near us.

Only when I enter the imaginative world of a story do I win

against the fear of war beginning again and destroying every-thing. Stories take me on an adventure and change my feelings, as though I am not me, but the main character in the story. I love becoming Sinbad, the fictional Arabian sailor. As I sail into mysteries, monsters hide everywhere, but I battle them and triumph, and always return home, bringing back gifts for everyone who waits for me.

I also triumph over fear by listening to old people tell of memories that bring peaceful, faraway worlds to me. I like how their faces light up when they describe the happy times of *hur-reyyah*, freedom. Their words give me hope and chase away my fears.